A HISTORY OF
PEWEE VALLEY

A HISTORY OF

PEWEE VALLEY

The Eden East of Louisville

DAVID RUSSELL
with
ALAN AXELROD

THE
History
PRESS

Published by The History Press
Charleston, SC
www.historypress.com

Front cover: Edgewood (formerly Sunnyside), with Alice Craig (Gatchel) at ease against a tree in the foreground. *Pewee Valley Historical Society.*

First published 2024

Manufactured in the United States

ISBN 9781467155083

Library of Congress Control Number: 2023938397

CONTENTS

AUTHOR'S NOTE

This book is built on the work of my late wife, Donna Andrews Russell (1954–2019), a journalist and marketing/public relations professional who was at heart an avid historian and historical researcher. She devoted untold hours to building and interpreting collections held by the Pewee Valley Historical Society, for whose generous cooperation in the making of this book I give my heartfelt thanks.

In 2014, Donna was honored by the Oldham County Historical Society as a Living Treasure in recognition of her work. She also was honored by the Kentucky Historical Society in Frankfort in 2017 for her volunteer service to the community. This award enabled the Pewee Valley Historical Society to win a state grant for the museum, which is to be named in her honor.

—*David Russell*
Pewee Valley

Chapter 1

WHERE IT'S AT AND WHAT IT IS

Let's begin with space and time. Pewee Valley is found at 38°18′34″ N 85°29′21″ W in Oldham County, Kentucky, United States of America, the world, the universe. Put another way, the town is centered on the intersection of LaGrange Road and Central and Ash Avenues and is just over the northeastern Jefferson County line in Oldham County, which puts it 18 miles northeast of Louisville. Per the U.S. Census Bureau, its total area is 1.9 square miles. The census bureau also tells us that, as of the 2020 census, 1,588 souls populated Pewee (estimated for 2023 at 1,665), which marks the highest count since the first census figures the bureau supplies, which are from 1890, when just 435 people were counted.[1]

Pewee Valley is overwhelmingly populated by U.S. citizens (98.4 percent). In fact, just 49 residents (that's 3.16 percent) were born outside the country. The median household income in 2020 was $113,333 and the median property value was $376,500, compared to $68,010 and $244,900 for the United States in general. Oh, and the median age of a Pewee Valley resident in 2020 was 48.5.[2]

So much for space and demographics. Let's tackle the dimension of time.

The site that is now Pewee Valley enters the historical record in 1784 as a four-thousand-acre land grant made by Virginia governor Patrick ("Give me liberty or give me death") Henry to Ora Norborn Beall. The most prominent early settlers were Michael and Rosanna Yager Smith, who came to Kentucky in 1807. Among their sons, one, Henry, was destined to become

Pewee Valley came of age with the railroad from Louisville. In 1909, when this photograph was made, downtown was dominated by tracks, a platform, and a depot—complete with fairytale gingerbread on its gables. *Pewee Valley Historical Society.*

the first among Pewee Valley's city fathers, starting in 1835 when he was commissioned to survey the road between Rollington and Floydsburg. That road became Pewee's Central Avenue.[3]

In 1849, trains began operating between the town of LaGrange and Louisville, and by 1852, several residences and summer homes had been built along the line. A stop, called Smith's Station, was established by the Louisville and Frankfort Railroad, and the community that continued to spring up around it took that name as well. Indeed, within a very few years of being dubbed Smith's Station, this little place became an artist colony and the seat of the Kentucky College for Young Ladies. By the end of the nineteenth century and into the early twentieth, Pewee Valley was a popular high-end resort and, thanks to its scenery and charming domestic architecture, was hailed as the most beautiful town in the state of Kentucky. Fortunately, much of this architectural heritage has not only been preserved but is lived in. Indeed, the town has long been the summer retreat of Louisville's elite families.

In 1895, author Annie Fellows Johnston published *The Little Colonel*, the first of thirteen children's books based on antebellum characters and locations in—you guessed it—Pewee Valley. The books enjoyed international success, culminating in the 1935 Fox Studio film *The Little Colonel*, starring

Shirley Temple, Lionel Barrymore, Hattie McDaniel, and Bill "Bojangles" Robinson, whose tap dance with little Shirley down a staircase is one of the iconic sequences in motion picture history—not to mention the first interracial dance ever shown to American film audiences.

THE SHOCKING MURDER OF NOBLE BUTLER'S BROTHER

Today an upscale metropolitan Louisville community, Pewee Valley also attracts many visitors, Kentucky locals and tourists alike. So, it's a real place with a real history. But it is also a legendary place, and the legend begins with one Noble Butler.

He was born on July 17, 1810, in Pennsylvania and, seven years later, moved with his family to what was then the midwestern frontier of Indiana. The Butlers eventually settled across the Ohio River in what is today Jefferson County, Kentucky. The seven-year-old began his education and did not stop until he graduated from Hanover, a Quaker college in Richmond, Indiana. That institution was so impressed by him that it named him chair of Greek and Latin. After three years, he moved to Louisville and opened a private school but was snatched up by the governing board of Louisville College, which hired him as a professor of ancient languages, and he went on to teach in several private schools.

Professor Butler was presented by Harvard College with an honorary Master of Arts in 1854. The scholar's rise was steady and his life happy until one day in November 1853, when his brother and fellow academic, William H. Gregg Butler, dared to reprimand a pupil, William Ward, for the crime of eating chestnuts in his Louisville High School classroom. Ward responded to the accusation by denying the deed, whereupon the pedagogue called him a liar and summarily whipped him.

On the next day, November 2, William and his brothers, Matt and Robert Jr., interrupted Professor Butler's lesson and demanded, in front of his class, an explanation for the accusation levied and the punishment meted out. An argument erupted, and Matt Ward drew a pistol, squeezed off a single shot and fatally wounded Butler, who died the very next day. After a sensational trial in April 1854, Ward was acquitted of a cold-blooded murder witnessed by an entire room full of his students.

WHAT'S IN A NAME?

Devastated following the murder, the trial, and what he called its "infamous verdict," Noble Butler left Louisville for the solace and solitude of what was then Smith's Station. Almost immediately on settling in the village with his family, Butler started calling the place Pewees Nest because eastern wood-pewee birds built a nest in the ruined cabin Noble sometimes used as his study.

Eastern wood-pewees are hardly imposing birds, described by one authority as "medium-sized flycatchers with long wings and tails." Sparrow-sized or smaller, pewees have short legs, an upright posture, and a peaked crown that imparts to the head a somewhat triangular shape. They are olive-gray with dark wings and an off-white throat and belly, as if wearing a vest. The underside of the pewee beak is yellow-orange. Butler made much of the song of the pewee, which, however, is little more than a single sustained one-note call followed by a rest and another call.[4]

By July 4, 1858, when Noble Butler published *Antiquitates Peweeji: A Discourse on the Antiquities of Peewee* [sic], crediting the work to "The Grand Panjandarum," Smith's Station had been firmly transformed into Pewee Valley.[5]

In twenty-three pages, Butler explained that the eastern wood-pewee is a mystical bird whose song—which sounds to him like "Pe-wee, Pe-wee…Peace and good will, peace and good will"—was premiered in no less a venue than the Creation, apparently God's way of celebrating that event. The pewee and its song vanished after Adam and Eve consumed the forbidden fruit and were thus cast out of Eden. The postlapsarian ages rolled by, millennium after millennium, until the "pioneer settlers" of the new Eden that would come to be called Pewee Valley "gathered themselves together, and erected those beautiful palaces which are the wonder of every passing traveler[,] and…learned the legend with which this veritable history commences."

These fortunate people "began to see that, segregated as they were from a barbarous world, they must make a government of their own, by which those who succeeded them might learn to be fitted for intercourse with the world outside. Pending the discussion of this weighty matter, there came another settler to these shores."

Whoever could that have been?

> *This was a scholar*
> *a bookman wise as three.*
> *Darker a scholar you shall not see*
> *In Jewrie, Rome or Araby.*

He was a man "modest of mien, but mighty in mind," who "placed his penates in an humble cottage, little dreaming the destiny fate had in store for him. To him had been committed, in the outside world, the charge of the barbarian youth." (Recall that, in 1839, Noble Butler became professor of Greek and Latin at the College of Louisville.) He was lured away from tutoring the "barbarian youth" when "his fancy wandered to the Arcadia of which he had heard from its pioneer settlers. Hither came he then, and in the little cottage sat him down to rest from toil. Foremost of all was he, this Professor, in framing the new government."

> *While sitting one day…"beneath the shady shadow of an umbrageous beech" contemplating the rules of all past governmental economy, as applicable to his new home, his ear was suddenly arrested with the magic sounds, "Pe-wee," "Pe-wee." At first he distrusted his hearing. Could it be the magic bird again had visited the earth? Was the promised paradise indeed renewed? Was "Peace and Good Will, Peace and Good Will," again to dwell in those shades where first it had been proclaimed? As thus, gazing upward, he enquired, the bird flew down and perched above his head, trilled forth the song of old, "Pe-wee, peace and good will; Pe-wee, peace and good will."*

The wise scholar "ran from house to house, and assembling his friends, he narrated his vision." His pioneer "friends" included Thomas Smith, a retired Lexington journalist and Louisville merchant, who built in 1856 Woodside Cottage, still standing in Pewee Valley's Central Avenue Historic District; W.C. Allen, an artist, whose portrait of Daniel Boone once graced Kentucky's old Capitol building; and Ben Casseday, who wrote *Casseday's History of Louisville* (1852) and lived at Owl's Nest in Pewee.[6] There was also Edwin Bryant, the second mayor of old San Francisco and the author of the best-selling *What I Saw in California*, the most authoritative guidebook used by the '49ers making their way to the California Gold Rush of 1848–49.[7] He returned from that Pacific El Dorado to Pewee, where he made his home in the rambling Oak Lea (also spelled Oaklea), which burned in May 1905.

Present as well were the widow (Patsy) and the daughter (Alice Estil Warfield) of former Virginia legislator Congressman Benjamin Estill, who died in 1853, just a year after moving to Pewee Valley. Finally, there was William D. Gallagher. A sometime poet and former editor of two literary journals—the *Cincinnati Journal* and, later, in Louisville, *The Hesperian*—and prominent editor of the *Louisville Morning Courier*, Gallagher lived in a Pewee property originally built of logs by James Alexander Miller in 1850. Miller called it Maple Nook, and Gallagher renamed it Undulata, after *Hosta undulata*, the wavy plantain lilies that apparently grew on the property when he bought it in 1852. Five years later, he built a second summer home on the property, Fern Rock Cottage.

Among the other members of the council Noble Butler described in *Antiquitates Peweeji* was the poet and novelist Catherine Anne Warfield, daughter of Sarah Percy and the first in a line of American authors in the Percy family, which included her sister Eleanor Percy Lee, William Alexander Percy (noted for *Lanterns on the Levee*, a 1941 bestseller), and the

Beechmore was built about 1830 by Michael Souther and his wife, Catherine. Her brother Joseph Clore bought the home in 1850 and subsequently sold it to the Warfields. Robert Elisha Warfield, a Lexington physician, had married sixteen-year-old Catherine Ware in 1833. They moved in 1860 to Beechmore, where Catherine, already known as an author, wrote her breakthrough Southern Gothic novel *The Household of Bouverie*. In 1896, Beechmore became the Jennie Casseday Rest Cottage for Working Women and, in 1946, the Mary A. Crain Private Hospital and Residence. It was destroyed in 1998 to make way for the Woods of Pewee Valley subdivision. *Pewee Valley Historical Society.*

much-esteemed Walker Percy, whose 1961 *The Moviegoer* won the National Book Award for Fiction. Catherine Anne Warfield, whose most memorable book was *The Household of Bouverie* (1860),[8] celebrated as the first Southern Gothic novel in American literature, lived in Pewee at Beechmore, a grand house that became the Mary A. Crain Private Hospital, located at the end of Rest Cottage Lane.

Catherine Anne Warfield provided yet another naming story for Pewee Valley in a poem she published in May 1873. Her version contends that the pioneers did hold council, which she sets in a "glade" that was "deeply emboweled"—yes, *emboweled*—"in a shade." They, too, soon reached a seemingly unresolvable deadlock. "Some amid ancient lore had sought" a name for their village:

> But the sounding titles of Greece and Rome
> Seemed strange in that peaceful, rural home.
> Grand Indian names some bore in mind,
> Strong and deep as the lurking wind,
> But they bore strange memories of whoop and yell,
> and were quite too fierce for that sylvan dell.
>
> Others had gathered from Spain and France,
> High sounding titles of past romance;
> And some had wished to enshrine the spot
> With the lovely legends of Walter Scott.

Alas, each suggested name "failed to please, and a silent cloud / Hung o'er the disappointed crowd; When suddenly from a tiny throat / Burst forth an unexpected, suggestive note."

> On the ledge of the porch where council met,
> Where his mate on her speckled eggs was set,
> While he hovered above her in loving glee—
> A self-called member proposed "Pee Wee."
> A sound of greeting—a glad "All Hail!"
> It seemed from the genies of the vale.

At this, a member of the council described only as "the dark browed student" but universally believed to be none other than Noble Butler addressed the bird directly: "You have supplied the wanted word." With that, "the council arose with one acclaim / And Pewee Valley became a name." As for the "the small, gray bird with marital nest," it remains today "Neath every roof...a welcome guest."[9]

HUMILIATION

Thus was the inauspiciously named village of Smith's Station mystically transformed by birdsong into a second Garden of Eden eighteen miles east of Louisville. From early on, this postage stamp of a town attracted prosperous Louisville merchants in search of country seats as well as a succession of writers, journalists, and artists in search of quiet inspiration. Yet not everyone was pleased with the name. The City of Pewee Valley was legally incorporated in 1870. A year later, on December 30, 1871, Louisville's *Courier-Journal* published a vignette titled "Country Seats. A Pen Picture of Pewee Valley." Its author, obviously a resident, bewailed the town's name as nothing less than "humiliating."

> *We seldom see anything about "Pewee" in your paper. Why is it? Have you forgotten us? Perhaps some of your readers do not know what a delightful, what a charming place Pewee Valley is; even one may exist who does not know where it is. This beautiful village lies on the edge of Oldham County, sixteen miles from the "Falls City," and, despite its name, is situated on a ridge which separates the waters of La Belle Riviere from those of the mighty and majestic Salt River. The cognomen is no longer appropriate to the flourishing and wide-spread town stretching out before the traveler whizzing by; but as it was given by a resident—a poet and a scholar—in honor of the little bird of the same name—neither a beauty or a sweet songster, but fond and familiar, coming through the house, assured of a welcome through the proverbial hospitality of the inmates—the town still bears the name, though humiliating.*

The humiliations kept coming. When the Jefferson Freeway, now part of I-71, opened in July 1969, the road sign indicating the Pewee exit misspelled the name as *Peewee*. The August issue of the local paper, *Call of the Pewee*, noted in a story titled "An 'E'asy Job" that the misspelling was duly "reported in *The Louisville Times*, and the Postmaster Matthews Fletcher wrote the state highway commissioner a letter of protest." The commissioner "promised to correct the error," and in the space of a month "the extra 'e' magically disappeared from the signs."[10] The magic lasted until 2003, when the Kentucky Transportation Cabinet reinserted the superfluous *e* on signs along I-71 between Louisville and I-75. Protests erupted, the offending vowel was removed a second time, and "Peewee" Valley was once again and forever more Pewee Valley.[11] Today, its residents celebrate their town's name and are grateful to have a home in so small but so enchanted a place.

Chapter 2

FIRST STOP, SMITH'S STATION

Noble Butler was not the first writer who claimed to have found a new Eden in Kentucky. Like Butler, John Filson (circa 1753–1788) started out his professional life as a schoolmaster. Legend has it that he gave up that calling shortly after fighting in the American Revolution because a battle wound to his arm impaired his ability to "properly thrash recalcitrant scholars." In 1783, the thirty-year-old Filson journeyed to Kentucky, where he invested in more than twelve thousand acres near Lexington and wrote his only book, *The Discovery, Settlement, and Present State of Kentucke* (1784), Kentucky's first history and one that also incorporates the first biography of its most celebrated early citizen, Daniel Boone.[12]

Admittedly, as an investor in "Kentucke" real estate, Filson, like Butler nearly a century later, was hardly an objective historian. Indeed, his book was more "promotional tract" than history. Yet his paradisal vision of the land does seem genuine. "When I visited Kentucke," he wrote, "I found it to far exceed my expectations." It was a "country…more temperate and healthy than the other settled parts of America," without the "sandy heats which Virginia and Carolina experience" in summer and with winters so mild that the "people are safe in bad houses; and the beasts have a good supply without fodder." As for Kentucky's settlers, they "are, in general, polite, humane, hospitable, and very complaisant."[13]

Filson's book was widely published and plagiarized, doubtless accelerating the settlement of Kentucky. By the early nineteenth century, this frontier state soon drew enough new residents to create one of the nation's earliest demands for rail transportation.

Just how early?

The world's first steam railroad was England's Stockton and Darlington Railway in 1825. Five short years later, the Baltimore and Ohio Railroad became the first railroad in the United States, and a year after that, in 1831, construction began (*in Kentucky!*) on the Lexington and Ohio. That railroad failed by 1840 and was sold to the state to satisfy debts but became the basis for the chartering and construction of the Louisville and Frankfort Railroad in 1847.[14]

In the meantime, in Oldham County, where today's LaGrange Road intersects with Central and Ash Avenues, settlers had established a community known as Rollington. It existed mainly as a stopping place for travelers between Louisville and Brownsboro and from Middletown to Westport. In 1851 construction of the L&FRR was completed. Its track ran for a ways alongside what became LaGrange Road, and in 1852, the railroad set up a stop about two miles southwest of Rollington. The company dubbed this stop "Smith's Station." Some believe it was named in honor of Thomas Smith, the president of the Louisville and Frankfort Railroad, but the *Encyclopedia of Louisville* holds that it was named after Henry S. Smith (no relation to Thomas), who was, as we will see, the nearest thing Pewee Valley has to a literal "city father."[15]

THE SMITHS

Rollington was one of two important pioneer settlements in what is now Oldham County. The other, Floydsburg, which first appears on a Jefferson County map in 1818, was likely the larger of the two, but Rollington began developing in the 1810s, more than half a century before Pewee Valley was incorporated. Pioneers purchased tracts of a four-thousand-acre land grant Norborn Beall had inherited from his father, Ora Norborn Beall. The 1820 census counted forty-five heads of households in Rollington, and in 1824, Silas Babbitt, a preacher and stonemason, aided by Bruce Jean, built Rollington's first church, Wesley Methodist Chapel. It was constructed of stone hauled in from the surrounding countryside. The chapel is about forty-four feet long and twelve feet high. The walls are two feet thick, the stones hand-hewn and fitted together without mortar. The rafters are of yellow poplar. This remarkable structure was used for services until 1892 and then became a one-room schoolhouse, drawing children from all over the area, who were educated there through grade eight. The longtime owners of the farm on which the building stands, the Haunz family, saw to it that the chapel remained intact, and it was placed in the National Register of Historic Places in 1984.[16]

There is also a record of a Baptist church having been started in the Rollington area in 1833. No trace of it remains, however, it having been dissolved—apparently—in 1836, "perhaps foreshadowing Rollington's later reputation for drinking and carousing!"[17]

No one could accuse the parents of Henry S. Smith, Michael and Roseanna, of carousing or, for that matter, of anything other than piety and hard work. They moved to Jefferson County, Kentucky, from Virginia in 1807 and settled near the Ohio River about twelve miles above Louisville. By 1819, Roseanna appeared on the rolls of the Harrod's Creek Baptist Church, which still stands today in Brownsboro, Kentucky. Son Henry married Susan Wilson (from New York) in 1836, and she joined Henry in membership at Harrod's Creek Church, Henry having been a member since October 16, 1824.[18]

Since 1830, Henry Smith had been doing surveying work for the Oldham County Court, and in 1835, he surveyed a road from Rollington to Floydsburg. He was also often hired to serve as an estate appraiser. He and his wife sold some of their Rollington property and moved to a farm situated between what is now Central Avenue and Huston/Houston Lane in Pewee Valley. By that time, the L&F was laying track during 1850–51, and much of it was alongside the road Henry Smith had surveyed. Railroad president Thomas Smith observed, "The land between the railroad and Rollington was in much demand for homes."[19]

Henry S. Smith, chief among Pewee Valley's founding fathers. *Pewee Valley Historical Society.*

Many of Pewee Valley's historic buildings— some built before, some after 1870, when Pewee Valley was named and then incorporated— were erected on Henry Smith's property north of LaGrange Road. These include an acre on Huston/Houston Lane, sold in 1856 to the L&FRR for the building of a section house (to house railroad workers), which was at the corner of Mount Mercy Drive. It survived until 2005, when it was demolished by the Pewee Valley Fire Department as a fire hazard beyond restoration. Also in 1856, the Smiths sold eight acres to

Thomas Marshall, trustee for his sister-in-law, Nannette B. Smith, the wife of Thomas Smith (again, no relation to Henry). This property included Woodside Cottage, where Thomas and Nannette lived. Built in 1856, it still stands in Pewee Valley's Central Avenue Historic District, having narrowly escaped destruction by fire in 1858, thanks to the "strenuous exertions of the neighbors," who managed to extinguish the blaze "before any great amount of damage was done."[20]

Before serving as president of the L&FRR, Thomas Smith had been the owner-editor of the *Kentucky Gazette*, which he purchased in 1809 when he was just twenty. Nannette was the cousin of Henry Clay Jr., son of Henry Clay, the "Great Compromiser," whose political maneuvering put off civil war for some years. The senior Clay served as a U.S. secretary of state, senator from Kentucky, and speaker of the House of Representatives. His son was killed in 1847 during the United States–Mexican War, and Nannette took in the son's three orphaned children (the junior Clay's wife having died in 1840). These two boys were subsequently killed in the Civil War, one fighting for the Union, the other for the Confederacy.[21] The Civil War divided American brother against American brother but nowhere more than in the border state of Kentucky. Today, Woodside Cottage is owned by St. Aloysius Catholic Church.

Another great house on the former Henry and Nannette Smith property, Bemersyde, is today one of the largest historic homes in Pewee Valley, with twenty-plus rooms.[22] As originally built, however, the house was much more modest. It was remodeled and enlarged by the Reverend Peyton H. Hoge in 1907, when he became pastor of Pewee Valley Presbyterian Church. Hoge had been pastor of Grace Mission (today Grace Covenant Presbyterian Church) in Richmond, Virginia, and then First Presbyterian Church in Wilmington, North Carolina, where he had succeeded no less a figure than Dr. Joseph R. Wilson, the father of future president Woodrow Wilson.

Hoge came to Pewee after resigning from Warren Memorial Presbyterian Church in Louisville and before answering the call to serve at the Presbyterian church in Princeton, New Jersey. Earlier in his career, when he was pastor in Wilmington, he performed a marriage ceremony in which the bride (a member of the church) was marrying a divorced man. Some considered Hoge's officiating to be blasphemous and blocked his succession to the position at Princeton church. Pewee Valley, always accepting of a generous degree of non-orthodoxy, welcomed Hoge with open arms. As for living at Bemersyde, the pastor accepted the extensive remodeling and enlargement of the house as a gift from no less a personage

Pewee Valley Presbyterian Church. *Pewee Valley Historical Society.*

than Henry Flagler, the oil baron and railroad developer who transformed Florida into a real estate bonanza.

Why was Flagler so generous to the reverend?

It may have had more than a little to do with Hoge's having officiated, in Florida, at the union of the seventy-one-year-old Flagler and the thirty-four-year-old Mary Lily Keenan after Flagler had divorced his second wife.[23]

THE BUILDING BOOM BEGINS

In 1858, a post office was built for Smith's Station, and that very same year, Nannette Smith's trustee, Marshall, bought another 3 acres from Henry and Susan Smith to add to Nannette's acreage. This land is the site of today's Pewee Valley Woman's Club and the Woodruff-Foley Brothers store. That same year, Henry and Susan sold 11⅜ acres to James A. and Mary Miller, who built a home on this property. It then became the site of the Mount Mercy Camp and Boarding School and is today the Mount Mercy Place subdivision. In 1861, William Alexander Smith, having married Mary Compton, bought 8 acres from his parents (Henry and Susan) and built a house sufficiently scaled to accommodate what became a family of eight children. The William A. Smith House still stands on its original 8 acres on Mount Mercy Drive.

Henry and Susan continued to sell in 1858, thereby further growing the town of Smith's Station. They sold twenty-one acres to Walter Haldeman (1821–1902), the founder and publisher of two iconic (alas, defunct since 1987) Louisville newspapers, the morning *Courier-Journal* and the afternoon *Louisville Times*. The brick Italianate home he built, Sunnyside, still stands, having been renamed Edgewood by Annie and Alexander (often called

The Mount Mercy Camp and Boarding School began life as the home of Judge William Henry Holt. In 1858, Holt sold it to James A. and Mary Miller, and later, the building became the nucleus of the Mount Mercy camp and school. Today, it is the site of the Mount Mercy Place subdivision. *Pewee Valley Historical Society.*

Aleck) Craig, who purchased it at auction for $13,900 on March 28, 1864. Haldeman, whose Civil War sympathies lay with the Confederacy, had left Smith's Station for Bowling Green, where he became the "official printer of the...Confederate 'shadow' government in Kentucky." He had left his wife, Elizabeth, and their children behind after transferring title to her. This legal step did nothing to deter the Union troops from seizing the property and auctioning it and other Haldeman assets.[24]

During the year following the end of the Civil War, 1866, Henry and Susan Smith purchased 220 acres adjacent to what was called the "Dulaney tract." Here, Woodford Hector Dulaney, a prominent Louisville businessman, transformed the many-porched cottage of Noble Butler into a substantially larger Gothic Revival summer home with flamboyant board-and-batten siding, Valentine-style gingerbread trim, and a steeply pitched gable roof. The ornate cottage was the perfect complement to the Dulaney mansion in Louisville. (That place was so immense that it was converted in 1924 into the Welsworth Hotel at Eighth Street and Broadway—"40 Rooms for Ladies and Gentlemen," every one of which came "with Lavatory" and was "Absolutely First Class.")

Even more appealing than the summer house itself were the grounds. In 1927, Melville Otter Briney interviewed (for the *Courier-Journal*) Woodford

Kate Matthews, Pewee Valley's most famous photographer, made this picturesque portrait of Tuliphurst, which took its name from the tulip trees that lined its walks and drives. *Pewee Valley Historical Society.*

Delaney's daughter Florence Dulaney Willis, who explained that her father "planted many of the wonderful trees from which the place takes its name of 'Tuliphurst,' and had the drives and walks laid off by some of the most distinguished landscape architects of the day. In the back of the estate, some distance from the house, is a spring of cold water that has been used ever since the house was occupied. The garden today is in the exact spot where the first flower garden was laid out, and surrounded by flowers of all kinds is a little sunken pool, and nearby a 115-year-old sundial taken from the farm of Judge Joseph Holt, Judge Advocate General in President Lincoln's Cabinet."[25] In 1955, J. Guy Pearson and his wife, Zella, developed the Tuliphurst subdivision on Dogwood Lane, using funds generated by the sale of lots to restore the Tuliphurst estate.[26]

CLOVERCROFT AND THE KENTUCKY COLLEGE FOR YOUNG LADIES

Clovercroft, located on Henry Smith's original holdings south of LaGrange Road, was built about 1866 by Milton M. Rhoher, who was the brother of Pewee Valley land speculator Jonas A. Rhohrer. Milton would serve as one of the seven original trustees of Pewee Valley when it was incorporated as a city in 1870. The Rhohers were in the second wave of early Pewee Valley settlers, just behind the Smiths, Haldemans, and Butlers.

Clovercroft had fourteen rooms and was designed in the popular Italianate style. Although it was lost to a fire on June 19, 1960, it is memorialized as the home of Katherine Marks, a featured character in Annie Fellows Johnston's "Little Colonel" series of books, all set in Pewee Valley. Marks was based on Kate Matthews, a pioneering female photographer who lived at Clovercroft until she died in 1956 and whose photographs illustrated the "Little Colonel" books as well as Johnston's autobiography. We will have much more to say about the "Little Colonel" and its connection to Pewee Valley in chapter 8.[27]

Like Clovercroft, the one-hundred-room Kentucky College for Young Ladies is gone today, a victim of a fire on August 28, 1900. The original structure was the heart of Willow Glen, a twenty-acre estate owned by Thomas Howell Crawford. Prominent in Louisville politics, Crawford was elected to that city's Board of Aldermen on the ticket of the notoriously nativist (anti-immigrant and anti-Catholic) Know-Nothing Party. He was elected mayor of Louisville in 1859 and served until April 6, 1861. In 1871,

Kate Matthews's double portrait of Gin and Sis Herdt at Clovercroft in 1928. *Pewee Valley Historical Society.*

Built about 1866, the fourteen-room Clovercroft was designed in the Italianate style popular in Pewee Valley and was immortalized as the home of Katherine Marks (the real-life Kate Matthews) in Annie Fellows Johnston's "Little Colonel" books. The house, alas, proved mortal, succumbing to fire on June 19, 1960. *Pewee Valley Historical Society.*

he became president of the Central Savings Bank of Kentucky. That same year, Crawford was one of the very first Kentuckians to install gas lighting, which he did at Willow Glen. On May 27, something went horribly wrong, there was a gas explosion, and both he and his sister-in-law were mortally injured. He lingered until June 17, but the house survived and was advertised for sale in the September 11, 1872 *Courier-Journal*: "very desirable…Price very reasonable."

On June 30 of the following year, the *Courier-Journal* published a story headlined "A NEW FEMALE SCHOOL":

> *Mr. Alfred E. Sloan, as principal teacher of the College Hill school for young ladies, situated near Cincinnati, and previously as the principal of a school at Danville, Kentucky, has during his years of service well merited the reputation of being one of the best educators in the West. Miss Lepha N. Clarke, as assistant to Mr. Sloan in the same school last year, and before that as the principle [sic] teacher in famous Vassar, is held at the front rank of her profession in America. She is a cultivated and elegant lady, with every evidence of possessing great firmness and the highest sense of duty. To these two—Mr. Sloan and Miss Clarke, with an able corps of experienced*

assistants—every encouragement has been given by the prominent residents of Pewee Valley, near Louisville, in the establishment of their new school in that pleasant town christened the "Kentucky College for Young Ladies" and to be opened the 10ᵗʰ of September next.

For the new school spacious and pleasant grounds have been secured in the charming town of Pewee, some sixteen miles from Louisville on the Short-line railroad, and the summer home of some of the wealthiest and most prominent gentlemen of Louisville. The town, in its appointments and surroundings, is probably the most attractive in Kentucky, within easy access of this city and its advantages, and just the place for the location of a female school. The college grounds embrace ten acres, well laid out, and said to be susceptible to the highest cultivation. The buildings are admirably arranged and commodious; formerly the country place of a wealthy Louisville gentleman, all the modern conveniences have been secured; the rooms are large and well-ventilated and newly furnished. The town itself is some 500 feet above the level of Louisville and is singularly healthy....

The students of the school will, naturally, come mainly from the South, and to the Southern parents the reputation of Mr. Sloan will commend it....Kentucky, the South and Louisville, in particular, are fortunate in the establishment of an institution which promises so much for the better education of their daughters.[28]

The "female school" did not take up the entire property. Pewee Valley First Baptist Church and Colored School was also located on the Willow Glen estate and was for a long time the second-oldest Black church in the area. Built under the auspices of the Reconstruction-era Bureau of Refugees, Freedmen, and Unclaimed Lands of Kentucky in the late 1860s, the church in turn provided a ninety-nine-year lease on a piece of land used to build a Black school. The Freedmen's Bureau oversaw construction, which cost exactly $292.50 in 1869.[29]

The Kentucky College for Young Ladies burned to the ground on August 28, 1900, and the First Baptist Church met the same fate much later, on August 17, 2003.

Pewee Valley Incorporated

Smith's Station, having begun as a mere railroad stop, at last acquired its own very fine gingerbread-adorned railroad depot, Pewee Valley Depot, in

1867. It accommodated both regular L&FRR service as well as a commuter service. The trains continued to run until 1933, when, the *Courier-Journal* reported, the "automobile put an end to [the depot's] usefulness." The depot was demolished in about 1960, having served for ninety-three years as "a symbol of what long time Pewee residents consider the Oldham County town's finest period—1867…through the early 1900s."[30]

Three years after the depot went into operation, in March 1870, the General Assembly of the Commonwealth of Kentucky passed "An Act to incorporate the Town of Pewee Valley, in Oldham County."[31] Henry Smith and the other men who were responsible for instigating the incorporation were appointed as the brand-new old town's first Board of Trustees on April 16, 1870.

As Henry Smith had done so much to bring Pewee Valley to life, so, too, in 1871, he collaborated with landscaper Stephen Schuler and other locals to develop Pewee Valley Cemetery as a place for its residents' final rest.[32] The cemetery also serves as a Confederate States of America Memorial and Veterans Burying Ground. Smith's own wife, Susan, died on August 26, 1871, and became the first known burial in the cemetery. Henry Smith followed her on March 18, 1883, and was laid to rest by her side.

Chapter 3

PEWEE PIONEERS, PART I

K entucky is a very American place, and it knows all about pioneers. It practically invented the pioneer prototype in Daniel Boone (1734– 1820), who, on the eve of American independence in 1775, blazed the trail known as the Wilderness Road. Through the Cumberland Gap, he led the first settlers into the Kentucky wilderness. Together, they planted Boonesborough, one of the very first English-speaking settlements west of the original colonies.

And it took off. Within twenty-five years, by the end of the eighteenth century, nearly a quarter million people had followed the route Boone pioneered. Pewee Valley was incorporated as a town by act of the Kentucky legislature on March 14, 1870, roughly ninety-five years after Daniel Boone breached that Cumberland Gap. This was the culmination of the labors of a new and different set of pioneers. They did not travel nearly so far but ventured just beyond the frontier of a teeming metropolis called Louisville. Their purpose was not to carve out of the wilderness another city but to make an alternative to the city, at the very least a part-time retreat from it in a little piece of Eden. These pioneers hewed out of the lush Kentucky forest…a *suburb*.

THE SUBURB: OLD SCHOOL

Truth to tell, American pioneers were never interested in creating anything really new. The places the Spanish conquistadors conquered they named after the cities and saints that had been familiar to them for centuries. The Pilgrims recycled all the names of the towns they knew, places like Plymouth and Boston, or they went back further and borrowed from the Bible. Louisville itself was named after King Louis XVI of France (reigned 1774–92) in honor of his having sent soldiers to fight in the American Revolution.

Nor did the Pewee pioneers invent the suburb. The word itself came from the Roman orator Cicero (106–43 BC), who called the great villas the patricians built on the outskirts of Rome *suburbani*. This classical model of suburban living comes close to what at least some of Pewee's pioneers envisioned for their little paradise. After the fall of Rome, the nature of suburbs changed. Throughout the so-called Dark Ages, suburbs were squalid places occupied mostly by the poor. By the eighteenth and nineteenth centuries, many wealthy and rising middle-class people craved refuge from cities that had become crowded, noisome, and generally unhealthy, especially in the heat of summer. The problem was that cities remained the centers of commerce, and commuting to your place of business on foot, on horseback, or even by carriage was not very practical.

Then came the railroad. Rail transportation developed slowly at first, but in 1825, soon after a steam engine was first mated to a locomotive, the world's first steam railroad, the Stockton and Darlington Railway, went into business in England. Four years later, Britain's George Stephenson built a steam locomotive he cannily named *Rocket*, and railroads began to appear throughout much of the world, including in the United States, where the Baltimore and Ohio, the nation's first railroad, started running in 1830. Just one year later, Kentucky climbed aboard with the Lexington and Ohio, which soon died aborning but did become the basis for the Louisville and Frankfort Railroad in 1847.[33]

Railroads made suburbs practical in many parts of the world, from London to Louisville. Commuting became a thing. As we saw in chapter 2, the locality that grew into Pewee Valley took root in the 1810s. Development of the area was accelerated by Pewee pioneers Thomas and Nannette Smith, who promoted settlement by buying and selling acreage substantial enough for respectable estates. When the tracks of the Louisville and Frankfort were laid alongside a road that Henry Smith had personally surveyed, the land he bought turned into gold and a building boom was underway. Daniel Boone had his Wilderness Road. Pewee Valley had the L&FRR.

A SPECIAL KIND OF BUILDING BOOM

Not all building booms are created equal. Immediately following World War II, as millions of GIs returned to civilian life, got married, and had families that started booming babies, the demand for housing soared. The automobile, which reached places the railroads did not, made the development of more and more suburbs possible. Across the nation, building booms mass-produced houses in the way that Henry Ford had mass-produced cars. The tract house suburban "bedroom community" was born. It served a purpose, and it became a white picket fence fixture of the American dream.

But it was very different from the dream of the Pewee Valley pioneers. The building boom the railroad spurred in Pewee Valley was no assembly-line operation. From the beginning, the place attracted people who were, in a word, uncommon. Some were Louisville's wealthiest and most prominent business and professional people, who could afford to build or buy exceptional homes, typically to get away from the city during the summer. But from the time that Noble Butler came to Pewee Valley in 1854, the locale also attracted artists, educators, and writers. The architecture both groups favored might be termed fanciful country Victorian, with steeply gabled roofs, elaborate board-and-batten siding, and loads and loads of gingerbread trim. These houses were generally built on ample acreage, which preserved the woodland aspects of the neighborhood. Gardens abounded, and they were almost always in the formally informal English style.

The pioneers presented in this chapter are mainly those who imparted to Pewee Valley during the antebellum years its enduring character. Many of these pioneers lived through the Civil War, when Kentucky, a so-called border state, which did not secede from the Union, was nevertheless deeply divided. Although some lived well beyond 1870, the personalities profiled in this chapter mostly settled here before Pewee Valley was incorporated by legislative act.

TWO MAYORS SLEPT HERE

Louisville mayors numbers 10 and 13 had homes in Pewee Valley. They may have had a short eighteen-mile train ride into the heart of the city, but in landscape, atmosphere, and even micro-climate, they were living in an idyll, to all appearances far removed from the bare-knuckles politics of a nineteenth-century American city.

John Barbee, tenth mayor of Louisville, owner of the Barbee House. Repeatedly remodeled and expanded through about 1910, it was later renamed Cedarhurst. *Pewee Valley Historical Society.*

Mayor #10, John Barbee, was born (September 16, 1815), lived, and died (December 22, 1888) in Pewee Valley. His father, James, built the family house about 1800, years before the area began to be developed in earnest. Between 1800 and about 1910, the Barbee house was rebuilt and added to until it ceased to be called either "Barbee House" or the "House of Mayor John Barbee" and instead was dubbed Cedarhurst. Still, its origin on the threshold of the nineteenth century makes it one of the earliest homes in the area, built by one of its first settlers. Indeed, when John Barbee was born in the house in 1815, he was among the first human beings to come into this world on this particular tract of land. If Henry Smith is the City Father in Chief of Pewee Valley, the Barbees could fairly be called its First Family.

Idyllic, even Edenic, early nineteenth-century Pewee Valley was not exempt from prevailing demographics. Calculated from birth, no country in the world had a life expectancy longer than forty years during the early nineteenth century.[34] By the time he turned eleven, John Barbee was an orphan. At fourteen, he had left the valley to find work in Louisville, where he found a job at Elisha Attry's dry goods store. He quickly took to the work, and in 1837, J. and J.W. Anderson hired him for their wholesale dry goods operation, the largest such store in Louisville. This position gave him a certain prominence in the commercial community, and in 1841, he was elected by the City Council to serve as collector of revenues for the Eastern District of Louisville.

He did not leap into public life with both his feet, however. In 1845, he left politics long enough to establish the wholesale dry goods house of Anderson, McLane, and Barbee. Later, he left that firm to partner in another dry goods enterprise with O. Brannin. He ran for City Council in 1849, won that year and again in 1851, serving as a councilman until he was elected Louisville's tenth mayor in 1855.

His opponent in that race was the incumbent mayor, a seasoned politician who was destined to become Abraham Lincoln's attorney general. But in the 1855 contest, James S. Speed, caught in a dispute over the expiration of his current term, did not declare his candidacy, let alone run a campaign. Backed by Louisville's Chancery Court, Speed contended that his mayoral term had not yet expired. This gave Barbee the edge. He ran on the ticket of the anti-Catholic, anti-immigrant Native American Party, better known as the "Know-Nothings" because members of this quasi-subversive nativist party invariably replied "I know nothing" when asked about the party's business. Knuckles were bared as the defeated Speed, a Catholic convert, disputed the election and sued in the Jefferson Circuit Court to overturn the results. The contentious case was ultimately settled in the State Court of Appeals, which, dominated by fellow Know-Nothings, decided in Barbee's favor.

Mayor Barbee served until April 6, 1857. The gravest crisis during his term was "Bloody Monday," August 6, 1855, when anti-immigrant and anti-Catholic elements clashed with Irish- and German-born residents on election day as they cast ballots for state officers and congressmen. That there were riots came as no surprise, but Barbee deliberately chose not to provide security at polling places. Know-Nothings attempted to stop naturalized Germans and Irish from voting. Many Germans were beaten and some killed in the East End and Butcher Town before the Know-Nothings moved on to the Eighth Ward to attack the Irish. Quinn's Row, a block of mostly Irish-occupied houses, was set ablaze, with loss of life. At last, Barbee acted, preventing his fellow party members from burning down the Catholic cathedral as well.

How very distant his tranquil Pewee Valley home must have seemed to the mayor on Bloody Sunday. He had married Eliza Kane in 1841, and the couple raised four children, Alice, Charlotte, Thomas, and John Jr., all in Pewee. Barbee did not run for another term as mayor but was elected to the City Council in 1858, serving until 1861. In 1860, he served as president of the Board of Councilmen. Barbee died at his Pewee home on December 22, 1888, but was buried at Cave Hill Cemetery in Louisville proper.

The thirteenth mayor of Louisville, Thomas Howell Crawford, held the office from 1859 to 1861. He was born a Virginian, the son of Thomas and Jane (Todd) Crawford, in Rockbridge County on March 1, 1803. We know the family came to Kentucky by 1809 because Crawford's mother had the dubious distinction of undergoing the world's first successful ovariotomy, performed on Christmas Day that year by the "father of the ovariotomy" and founding father of abdominal surgery, Dr. Ehpraim McDowell, who practiced in Danville, Kentucky. The tumor he removed, without benefit of either anesthesia or sterile surgical conditions, weighed seven pounds. Jane Todd Crawford? She went on to live into her seventy-eighth year.

In 1857, Thomas Crawford was elected to the Louisville Board of Aldermen, like Barbee, on the Know-Nothing Party ticket. He served as the board's president for half of 1858 and went on to be elected mayor of Louisville on April 2, 1859, serving until April 6, 1861. A passionate supporter of the North during the Civil War, he ran again for mayor in 1863 on the Union ticket but lost to William Kaye, whose enthusiasm for the Union was sufficiently tepid to earn him the support of Louisville's substantial secessionist faction.

Crawford was a prosperous real estate agent during the mid-1860s, and in 1870, he was also an agent for the Piedmont and Arlington Life Insurance Company of Virginia. By this time, he also served as president of the Central Savings Bank of Pewee Valley.[35]

It is not clear when Crawford built his country villa in Pewee. Called Willow Glen, it was sited on twenty acres and was one of the grand homes visible from the Pewee Valley Train Depot, as noted in an anonymous *Louisville Courier-Journal* story called "Country Seats: A Pen Picture of Pewee Valley," published on December 25, 1871. Willow Glen, according to the article, was near Clovercroft, "the picturesque Italian villa of Milton Rhorer," and "'Valhalla,'…the rural retreat of…J.M. Armstrong."[36]

KENTUCKY COLLEGE FOR YOUNG LADIES, PEWEE VALLEY, KY.

An engraving of Kentucky College for Young Ladies. Like so many classic Pewee Valley structures, it was destined for a fiery death. *Pewee Valley Historical Society.*

Willow Glen was likewise picturesque but also thoroughly modern. Crawford was among the very first Kentuckians to install gas lighting in his home. Tragically, that installation proved to be far from perfect. On May 27, 1871, the lighting mysteriously failed, and Crawford and his sister-in-law Matilda G. Martin descended into the cellar to see if they could locate the problem. Since the gaslights were out, they each carried a lighted candle. As they opened the cellar door, an explosion was ignited, killing Matilda outright and injuring Crawford so gravely that he died three weeks later.

Willow Glen, remarkably, survived and, following extensive expansion, went on to a new life as the Kentucky College for Young Ladies, which awarded its first diplomas in 1873. The school was financed by Louisville businessmen John G. Barrett, John T. Moore, Colonel W.A. Meriwether, and J.B. Kinkead, among others, who saw the institution as a means of improving the "cultural advantages of our city and State."[37] The college was celebrated in verse by W.D. Gallagher (1801–1894), one of Pewee Valley's early literary residents, whom many considered the "resident poet" of their Eden:

"THE PLANTING OF THE TREE"

I.

Plant, plant the tree of Youth!
Water it with tears of gladness;
Train it in the forms of truth,
That it will bear not fruit of sadness;
Tend it well through all the years,
All the seasons, all the hours—
Seeing that no worm appears
In the fruit or on the flowers.

II.

Plant, plant the tree of Love!
Nourish it with fervent feeling—
Day by day the vow above
Recorded, sealing—newly sealing;
And as roll the years away,
Doubt not ever—never falter—
Not ev'n for a moment stray
From the faith that bless'd the alter [sic].

III.
Plant, plant the tree of Life!
God will help you watch and tend it,
So that all earth's storm and strife
Can not either break or bend it.
Fix your thoughts and hearts above,
Where the anthems still are ringing.
"Christ is risen!" "God is love"
Which the angel hosts are singing.

What little fame Gallagher may have earned as a poet has dimmed, but he did merit an entry in E.A. and G.L. Duyckinck's *Cyclopedia of American Literature* (New York: Charles Scribner, 1856; 2:471–72) and inclusion in Edgar Allan Poe's 1841 "A Chapter on Autography." Poe was not only a poet, writer of gothic tales, and essayist, but he also edited a variety of journals and magazines. He therefore read a great many manuscripts submitted by writers and would-be writers, and he judged not only their literary merits but the quality of their "autography" (handwriting):

> *Mr. GALLAGHER is chiefly known as a poet. He is the author of some of our most popular songs, and has written many long pieces of high but unequal merit. He has the true spirit, and will rise into a just distinction hereafter. His manuscript tallies well with our opinion. It is a very fine one,—clear, bold, decided and picturesque. The signature above* [it was reproduced in the magazine] *does not convey, in full force, the general character of his chirography* [handwriting], *which is more rotund, and more decidedly placed upon the paper.*[38]

While Gallagher's verse celebration of the Kentucky College for Young Ladies survives, the college itself burned to the ground on August 28, 1900, having graduated its last class in June of the preceding year.[39]

Chapter 4

PEWEE PIONEERS, PART II

Pewee Valley pioneer Noble Butler was not alone in believing he had found a new Earthly Paradise. But for many mid-nineteenth-century Americans, Eden ran a distant second to California. Pewee Valley is 2,210 miles (via today's I-80) east of Sutter's Mill, where gold was discovered in 1848. Nevertheless, it was one of Pewee's most interesting pioneers who played a key role in the California Gold Rush of 1849.

THE PEWEE PIONEER WHO STRUCK IT RICH IN CALIFORNIA

Edwin H. Bryant was a Yankee from Pelham, Massachusetts, born on August 21, 1805. He became a newspaperman, starting up the *Literary Cadet* in Providence, Rhode Island, before moving to Rochester, New York, as editor of the *New York Examiner*. In 1830, he accepted the invitation of George D. Prentice to become coeditor with him of the *Louisville Journal* and settled in Kentucky. When the *Journal*'s owners decided they couldn't afford two editors, Bryant moved in 1831 to Lexington, where he was instrumental in founding the *Lexington Observer* and *Lexington Intelligencer*. In 1832, he and a partner purchased the *Kentucky Reporter* from Thomas Smith, a Lexington editor. In 1844, after two years on the *Reporter*, Bryant left Lexington and returned to Louisville at the behest of Walter Haldeman, who would also go on to become a Pewee pioneer. Haldeman had just taken over a fledgling newspaper, the *Louisville Daily Dime*, which soon morphed into the *Louisville Morning Courier*.

In 1846, suffering from what the historical record describes only as "poor health," Bryant availed himself of what was perhaps nineteenth-century medicine's favorite prescription: a change of climate. He left Louisville on April 18, 1846, bound overland for California. It was one of those arduous cures that would likely kill you if it didn't make you better. He traveled to Independence, Missouri, the hub for overland covered wagon-train travel, and joined a large train, which included the soon-to-be-infamous Donner Party. The Donners were fans of Lansford W. Hastings's *Emigrants' Guide to Oregon and California*. Published in 1845, it was a shameless promotional tract masquerading as an objective guidebook. With an air of authority, Hastings advocated leaving the well-traveled Oregon Trail "about two hundred miles east of Fort Hall; thence bearing west-south west, to the Salt Lake; and thence continuing down to the bay of San Francisco."[40] The trusting Donners blithely obeyed. On June 27, the wagon train paused to camp at Fort Bernard, Wyoming Territory. There, a well-known seasoned mountain man, James Clyman, warned the travelers in no uncertain terms to avoid the "Hastings Cutoff" and stick to the Oregon Trail instead. The Donners politely declined the advice, but Bryant and eight others heeded Clyman.

The result?

The Donner Party found itself hopelessly snowbound in the Sierra Nevada, started to starve, and resorted to cannibalism. Bryant and his traveling companions, on the other hand, safely reached Sutter's Fort, California, on September 1, 1846.

Bryant did not remain in California for long, departing in June 1847, but he packed an awful lot into his stay. He traveled more than five hundred miles south, as far as San Diego, then turned around and returned to San Francisco, where U.S. Army general Stephen Watts Kearney—having carried out President James K. Polk's order to "conquer and take possession of California" from Mexico—appointed him the second *alcalde* (mayor) of that city. In the five months during which he served, Bryant arranged the sale of 450 publicly owned waterfront lots to private buyers, purchasing 14 for himself. He paid a total of $4,000 and flipped them in 1849 for $100,000 (nearly $4 million today). San Franciscans named a street after him.

During his travels, Bryant never forgot that he was a journalist. He kept meticulous notes, returned with Kearny's party to the East, and rapidly wrote a book he titled *What I Saw in California*. It was published early in 1848, in ample time for the height of the gold rush. The book was an immediate bestseller, going through many editions in 1849 and after. Bryant did what Hastings had failed to do: give valuable, accurate, and prudent information, especially concerning routes and supplies. As a bonus, he included a sensational account of the Donner Party tragedy as a cautionary tale.[41]

Bryant dashed back to California in 1849 to close his real estate sale and collect his cash and then returned to Kentucky, where he settled in Pewee Valley, on an estate called Oak Lea (sometimes spelled as one word, Oaklea), which was located on what is today called Muir's Lane. Oak Lea soon became known as the venue for "many a gay party."[42] No doubt! Between his timely California real estate investments, his book royalties, and his popular *What I Saw in California* speaking tours, Edwin Bryant became a wealthy man. In his *Antiquitates Peeweeji*, Noble Butler gives him a prominent place in the pantheon of Pewee's literary and artistic pioneers:

> *There was in those days a mighty traveler—One of those "pioneers of modern civilization," as they are called by the barbarians without—who had founded a new empire upon the shores of the distant Pacific; who had led her serried hosts across the burning plains of America, to the gold bearing regions of the modern El Dorado, and who, despising the yellow dross he trod beneath his feet, contented himself with bringing the blessings of law and order; with possessing himself corner-lots and the affections of his people; till, from the revolution he effected there has grown an empire that, in no small degree, governs the world. Did he remain to be Emperor of the land he had won from the savage? Marius perished amid the ruins of Carthage; Columbus died requesting that the manacles, with which he had been dishonored, might be buried with him; Pizaro [sic] was assassinated at the apex of his glory; but the Lord High Chancellor of Pewee [i.e., Edwin Bryant] lived to be one of the founders of the most glorious kingdom known to man; and still lives to bless it with his wisdom and to feed it from his larder.*[43]

From all appearances, Edwin Bryant led a charmed life, which was crowned with extraordinary financial success. It was for that very reason that the December 17, 1869 *Courier-Journal* published this account of his demise the day before under the headline "A Shocking Death":

> *Fall of Judge Edwin Bryant from the Third Story of the Willard Hotel. The city was shocked yesterday by the announcement of the sudden and terrible death of Judge Edwin Bryant. Judge B. lived in Pewee Valley,*

but, suffering from bad health came to the city [Louisville] *about three weeks ago and placed himself under the treatment of his physician. He was staying at the Willard Hotel, and occupied room No. 31 on the third story. Yesterday morning about half-past six o'clock while his servant was absent from the room, and while, it is supposed, he was laboring under a fit of temporary insanity, he got out of his bed, and, opening the window, jumped out, falling to the pavement below, in the backyard, a distance of fifty or sixty feet. He was severely bruised internally by the fall and lived no more than half an hour afterward.*

Judge Bryant was sixty-two years of age.[44]

Bryant's Pewee Valley home, Oak Lea, was not long vacant. Peter Brown Muir, a native of Bardstown, Kentucky, born on October 19, 1822, became a distinguished jurist who graced the Louisville bench for many years and simultaneously held a professorship at the law school of the University of Louisville. In June 1870, he left both the judiciary and academia to move to Pewee Valley and enter private practice in Louisville with Martin Bijur and George M. Davie. He subsequently cofounded the firm of Muir & Heyman. It wasn't that Judge Muir had grown weary of the public sector. He had what the Family Search website calls "at least" six sons and six daughters[45] and clearly needed to make more money and own a big house. In the year of his move, he purchased Oak Lea from St. James Episcopal Church minister Reverend George D. Cummins, who had acquired it from the Edwin Bryant estate the year before.

Judge Peter Brown Muir was the model for the fictional Judge Moore of "Little Colonel" fame. In real life, he was instrumental in the incorporation of Pewee Valley as a city and wrote the founding charter for the Pewee Valley Cemetery Company. *Pewee Valley Historical Society.*

Muir deserves to be called a City Father because he made use of his legal and political skills, as well as his reputation, in service to the newly incorporated Pewee Valley as first president of the city's Board of Trustees, an office he would hold for fourteen years. Muir also wrote the charter for the Pewee Valley Cemetery Company, which was incorporated by act of Kentucky law on March 6, 1872.

On March 26, 1885, Judge Muir's wife, Sophronia, died from burns sustained after her clothing caught fire when she stood too close to a fireplace while dosing herself with medicine, likely alcohol- or turpentine-based. Muir resigned from the Pewee Valley Board of Trustees on November 28, 1889, when he moved to the home of his daughter and son-in-law, Belle and Harry Weissinger, in Louisville. He did live to see Pewee Valley prosper and the Pewee Valley Cemetery become a prominent fixture in the town. In 1904, the company he chartered assigned 11,275 square feet of the cemetery to the Kentucky Confederate Home, which maintained it as the Confederate Burying Ground. Here rest the remains of 313 men, most of whom died while in residency at the Confederate Home. To this day, the cemetery is Kentucky's only official resting place for Confederate troops.

Although he took up residence with his daughter and son-in-law in Louisville, he continued to summer in his Pewee Valley home. He rallied to the aid of the city in 1902 in a vain effort to block the Kentucky Confederate Home from relocating in the then-vacant Villa Ridge Inn. He appealed to Governor John Crepps Wickliffe Beckham to stop the move, but Beckham declined to intervene. Perhaps by way of consolation, Beckham appointed the judge's son Upton to the Court of Common Pleas. As for poor Oak Lea, it suffered another fire on May 26, 1905, an event that warranted substantial coverage in the *Louisville Courier-Journal* on May 27:

> *Dinner had just been served when Peter B. Muir, Jr., the five-year-old son of Mrs. Upton Muir, ran down stairs crying and said the house was on fire. He was not believed at first, but when he wailed loudly a servant ran up stairs and found the house full of smoke. A few minutes later flames broke out under the room. The cry of fire broke out over the little town and the town bell was rung. Soon a crowd of 500 persons had gathered at the scene of the fire and the men busied themselves carrying out everything that they could reach. (Editor's note: Pewee Valley's entire population was under 500 in 1900. Many of the people at the fire had to have been inmates of the Kentucky Confederate Home, which had opened three years before across Muirs Lane from Oaklea. Did they know how vigorously the good judge opposed the home a few years earlier?) As the fire was in the roof and it had not gained much headway when it was discovered, the volunteers had much time at their disposal in carrying the furniture from the lower level....*

> SAVED THE DOORBELL.
> *On account of the zeal of those who rushed to the fire to save something, many ridiculous incidents resulted. One man took an ax, and while a large*

crowd looked on in interest, chopped away the wood about the handle of the front door bell and carefully took it out of danger from the fire. The kitchen stove, with the fire in it and the bread still baking in the oven, was carried out in the yard. Many of the window sashes and the panes were taken out, and some of the woodwork of the house was saved.

The burned-out Oak Lea was replaced by a brand-new Oak Lea, built in the Colonial Revival style on the existing foundation. Judge Muir owned that house until his death in 1911, when it passed to members of his family. After his passing, Oak Lea Road was renamed Muir's Lane.

PAINTER AND WRITER

Pewee Valley attracted the prosperous and the artistic, who, more often than not, were not one and the same. Among the first artists to come to the valley was Carl Christian Brenner. Born in Lauterecken, Kingdom of Bavaria, in August 1838, he was educated in the public schools through the age of fourteen. At least one of his teachers was sufficiently perceptive to realize he was in the presence of a budding talent and, through contacts, secured support from no less than "Mad King" Ludwig II of Bavaria to gain Brenner admission to the Academy of Fine Arts in Munich. Brenner's future as an artist looked golden until his father refused permission for his enrollment and instead trained the boy as a glazier, a trade he assumed (not without good reason) would be more profitable than artist.

The Brenners immigrated to the United States in 1853, settling briefly in New Orleans before moving to Louisville in the winter of 1853–54. Young Brenner found work as a glazier as well as a house and sign painter. Despite his lack of formal training in fine art, he won a commission from the Louisville Freemasons in 1863 to paint panoramic views of Civil War battles. This earned him local fame, and in 1867, he was able to open a studio on Louisville's Jefferson Street.

By 1871, he was a full-time artist, specializing in landscapes, and was soon widely deemed the greatest artist in the state. He was an early exponent of Tonalism, a landscape style that was moody, dark, and highly atmospheric. Among the best-known Tonalists were James McNeill Whistler, George Inness, Albert Pinkham Ryder, and John Henry Twachtman, all numbered among the great or near-great. Though largely forgotten today, Brenner was painting in the Tonalist style well before any of these men.

Brenner exhibited at the Louisville Industrial Exposition (1873) and gained national recognition after being shown at the Pennsylvania Academy of Fine Arts in 1876. He was inducted into the National Academy of Design in 1877 and remained very active until 1886. Two years after he retired, he died in Louisville on July 22, 1888.

While he earned fame on a national scale, Brenner was most celebrated for his detailed landscapes of scenes in Pewee Valley as well as Louisville's Cherokee Park. He never tired of painting beech tree landscapes, especially in the somber light of winter. In a 1979 *Louisville Courier-Journal* article, Jean Howerton Cody wrote of how Brenner "would set up his easel and a folding chair in a portable hut with large glass exposures and paint away in rain or snow." In a later *Courier-Journal* article, Diane Heilenman depicted him as a fixture of nineteenth-century Pewee Valley: "Wearing his artist's hat and carrying a staff and a paint box, Brenner was a familiar figure in Louisville parks and Pewee Valley woods."[46]

As Carl Christian Brenner was a pioneer Pewee Valley painter, so Catherine Anne Warfield (1816–1877) was one of its earliest notable writers. She was born Catherine Ware in Natchez, Mississippi, and, with her younger sister Eleanor, grew up in Philadelphia, Pennsylvania, where her mother struggled to recover from the severe post-partum depression that followed Eleanor's birth. As young women, both Catherine and Eleanor wrote and published poetry, even collaborating on two books, *The Wife of Leon* (1843) and *The Indian Chamber* (1846). In 1833, when she was sixteen, Catherine married Robert Elisha Warfield, son of a well-known Lexington, Kentucky, physician and breeder of Thoroughbreds. Catherine and her husband lived in Lexington and wintered in Natchez. They left Lexington in 1857 after suffering financial reverses and moved to Beechmore, a large house in Pewee Valley, which was demolished in 1998 to make way for the Woods of Pewee Valley subdivision during a more recent period in Pewee Valley's suburban development.

By the mid-1850s, Catherine had turned from poetry to fiction, becoming a prolific novelist. Her most successful work, *The Household of Bouverie* (1860), was written while she lived at Beechmore. A lurid and commercially successful gothic tale, the novel is about a young orphan who comes from England to live with her grandmother in America. Here, in her grandmother's house, she accidentally discovers—wait for it—her grandfather! Holed up in a secret room on the second floor of the house, the old man, Erastus Bouverie, long presumed dead, lives as a reclusive madman, occupying himself in a search for a potion he hopes will restore his youth. He and the orphaned girl grow close to one another, and through him, the orphan discovers her family's dark history.[47]

Despite their straitened finances, the Warfields became the center of "an attached circle of artists, poets, editors, and other persons of culture. Among her immediate neighbors [were] Edwin Bryant…; Noble Butler, the accomplished scholar, critic, grammarian, and teacher; [poet] William D. Gallagher, and others of like tastes, cultivation, and pursuits."[48]

Elisha Warfield died in 1872, and Catherine followed five years later. Both are buried in Lexington Cemetery, Lexington, Kentucky. Catherine (as her last will and testament records) left "my place Beechmore" to "my sons Nathaniel and Lloyd Warfield with their families." As Catherine noted in the will, however, Beechmore was encumbered by a mortgage. Ultimately, Nathaniel and his wife, Alice, lived out their lives in Pewee Valley, occupying another house they built on the Beechmore estate.

Although Catherine Warfield's novels are little read today, she and her sister Eleanor were the first published authors of what became a celebrated American literary family. Their mother was born Sarah Percy. Her relation William Alexander Percy (1885–1942) wrote a best-selling autobiography, *Lanterns on the Levee*, in 1941. When his first cousin LeRoy Pratt Percy and his wife, Martha Susan (Mattie Sue) Phinzy Percy, were killed in a car accident, William adopted their three children, one of whom was Walker Percy (1916–1990). Walker grew up to become the author of several distinguished novels, including *The Moviegoer* (1961), which won the National Book Award for Fiction.[49]

We have Catherine Warfield to thank for this word portrait of Pewee Valley as it existed in antebellum Kentucky. This piece appeared in the *Louisville Democrat* on March 19, 1856:

> *HABITS, MANNERS AND CUSTOMS OF THE PEWEE NATION—COACHES, DOCTORS, POST OFFICES, CHURCHES, ETC., ETC.*
>
> *Messrs. Editors: This celebrated valley is situated on a ridge. It is about 16 miles from Louisville, on the railroad between Frankfort and that place. I will say nothing, of course, about the train leading to such an important place, it must be of the best order, and the genuine politeness of the conductors is well known to all who have ever travelled that road— they seem to be preparing you for the cordial reception you will meet when you arrive at Pewee. So much has been said of the various beauties and pleasures of this place, that my readers will have to excuse me if I fail to give them anything original. With this apology, I will proceed.*

The place does not attract attention on account of its longstanding—for it has been but lately settled—but for the new and startling ideas which it has originated. It is really true—however much the assertion may be doubted—that Peweeans have discovered it is possible to dance in calico dresses and ride in a one-horse sleigh. For fear our readers will suppose we are imbibing Hottentotish ideas, I will tell them that we should be perfectly willing to ride in a four-horse sleigh with buffalo robes, bells &c.; but we should not refuse a one-horse one, without the supposed necessary appendages, if the former were unattainable. Not the least pleasure of the sleigh rides were the upsets, and they were not unfrequent either, for it was very seldom that a party returned without having had an affectionate embrace with mother earth.

I think it must be the nature of a Peweean to love sleigh riding, for they practiced it perseveringly even after the snow had bid farewell. But, perhaps, some reader will remark that it is because they have no other vehicle. Now I beg leave to inform that person that he is mistaken, because we have others. Yes, the equipages of Peweeans are well known to all its visitors; but for fear you should know none of these visitors, I will tell you what they are: CARTS!—but you had better not call them so to a Peweean, here they are carriages—very good carriages, too—and if you don't happen to sit over the wheels, you will ride very smoothly. Oh! It is enough to stir the hearts of the lookers-on (and the bodies of the riders) to see with what independence of character the Peweeans mount their carriages and roll off amidst the astonished gaze of all those who happen to be in the railroad cars.

As you descend from the cars, you find yourself upon a large platform, with a small white house before you. This is the station, store and post office of Pewee Valley. My heart swells with pride as I write the word POST OFFICE, as should every Peweean's who is anxious for the prosperity of his country, home, village—I don't know what to call it; for it is too small to be called CITY, and too important to be called village.

It is principally on account of this post office that I write this letter; for I think it is my duty to encourage the advancement of this place; and though my fingers tremble at the idea of these words appearing before the public, I still write on. The first house you perceive is Woodside Cottage, embowered by the tall trees, through which the summer sun steals and falls in broken fragments on the emerald grass.

As you look at its white walls gleaming amid the dark green leaves, you cannot help thinking it was one of the houses built by the fairies in olden

The unassuming Pewee Valley Post Office was a source of great pride to residents of the village. *Pewee Valley Historical Society.*

times for their especial favorites. Not that it looks in the least antiquated, though, for it was built only a short time ago. The next house you come to is not celebrated for its beauty or singularity of architecture, but for a pair of ferocious dogs who never fail to welcome all passers-by and the effect of the meeting is really very "moving."

Then comes Tuliphurst, the residence of Mr. Butler, who is so popular on account of his sociability and talents, that the inhabitants have placed him in the elevated position of King of Pewee Valley. The house abounds in little porches, which suggests how pleasant it must be to sit on them of a summer's evening. Next is the Doctor's house, which looks very comfortable, but still seems to want a female's hand about it. The others are Vinona, Tangle-Dell, Owl's Nest, and Undulata. The latter is the home of Mr. Gallagher, the poet. A more appropriate name could not have been chosen, and it shows Mr. Gallagher appreciated the singular beauty of the place when he named it.

On a hill a little beyond Mr. G's is our church. We have a pulpit and a library, and I am anxiously awaiting a time when we shall have backs to our seats; but this is only when I am not there, for when listening to the eloquent sermons Mr. Wallace preaches every other Sunday, all discomforts are forgotten. There are no trees directly around the church, for we have to afford room for the numerous sleighs, CARRIAGES and horses that arrive after church, to talk while our gallants are preparing our CARRIAGES; and then we drive merrily home. It is not unusual for the lady to take the reins in her own hand, if she wishes to go, and has no gentleman to take her.

The guest of one is the guest of all in this delightful valley; and we have a welcome for all who come, provided they leave city airs behind them.

Long life to Pewee and may it ever prosper![50]

Chapter 5

THE CIVIL WAR COMES TO PEWEE

As most folks see it, the Civil War was all about South versus North, "slave" states versus "free." But the truth was not nearly so tidy. Eleven states, all southern slave states, did eventually secede from the Union, but there were also so-called border states, which were slave states that did not secede. These were Delaware, Maryland, Missouri, and Kentucky. West Virginia was a special kind of border state. When Virginia left the Union, its western counties seceded from the rest of Virginia and were ushered into the Union on June 20, 1863, as West Virginia, a brand-new slave state loyal to the Union.

A STATE DIVIDED

Representatives from the first secessionist states convened in Montgomery, Alabama, on February 8, 1861, and declared themselves the Confederate States of America. Jefferson Davis of Mississippi was elected president and Alexander Stephens of Georgia vice president. Yet there were those in the North who remained hopeful that war could still be averted and the Union glued back together. One of these hopeful men was John J. Crittenden, senator from Kentucky. Born in Versailles, Kentucky, in 1787, he was the son of the Revolutionary War major after whom he was named. He not only wanted to preserve Kentucky for the Union, but he also wanted to preserve the Union.

As early as December 1860, while Abraham Lincoln's predecessor, James Buchanan, was still in the White House, Crittenden presented six constitutional amendments that would effectively revive the defunct Missouri Compromise of 1820 and extend the line dividing slave states from free states all the way to the Pacific. In addition, the federal government would see to the strict enforcement of the Fugitive Slave Law and would even indemnify owners of fugitive slaves whose return was prevented by antislavery elements in the North. Popular sovereignty—the right of the population of each new state added to the United States to vote itself slave or free—would be extended to all the territories, and slavery in the District of Columbia was to be protected from congressional action.

President Buchanan said nothing about the Crittenden Compromise, and President-elect Lincoln declined to address the proposal directly but did tell a Republican colleague to "entertain no proposition for a compromise in regard to the extension of slavery." This was sufficient to deliver a mortal wound to the proposal. In January 1861, Crittenden tried to get a public hearing on the compromise and introduced a resolution calling for a national referendum on his proposals. The Senate never took up the resolution.

But Crittenden did not give up. Not only was he determined to prevent the nation and his state from being torn apart, he was also desperate to hold his own family together as well. As a Kentucky father, he knew firsthand that the Civil War would ultimately pit brother against brother. His son George Bibb Crittenden made it clear that he intended to side with the Confederacy. His other son, Thomas Leonidas Crittenden, was as adamant about joining the Union cause. When war broke out, George became a Confederate general and Thomas a Union general.

In the era of Buchanan and Lincoln, Inauguration Day was in March, and, on March 2, 1861, just two days before the ceremony, Senator Crittenden's proposal for a set of amendments protecting slavery in exchange for loyalty to the Union was narrowly defeated in the Senate.

With compromise defeated, Kentucky did not leave the Union but did declare itself neutral as soon as the war broke out. Nevertheless, from the beginning, Kentuckians fought on both sides, and official neutrality did not last long. North Carolina–born Leonidas Polk, like Crittenden the son of a Revolutionary War officer, was a graduate of West Point, receiving his commission as a U.S. Army second lieutenant on July 1, 1827. On December 1 of that year, he resigned that commission to study theology at Virginia Theological Seminary. He was soon ordained as an Episcopal priest. By the outbreak of the Civil War, he was bishop of the Louisiana Convention and summarily pulled the convention out of the Episcopal Church of the United States and into the Protestant Episcopal Church in the Confederate States of America, which he had just created. His hope was that secession would bring a peaceful separation of the slave states from the United States, but he nevertheless wrote to his friend and former West Point classmate, now president of the Confederate States of America, Jefferson Davis to offer his services to the Confederate army. Asked if he was taking off his bishop's gown to take up a general's sword, he replied, "No, Sir, I am buckling the sword over the gown."

With no more military experience than that of second lieutenant, General Polk was commissioned a major general on June 25, 1861, and dispatched to command the region between the Mississippi and Tennessee Rivers. In September, he deployed troops to occupy Columbus, Kentucky. It was a colossal blunder, which prompted the state legislature to override the governor's neutrality policy by asking the U.S. government to send troops to "expel the invaders." Ultimately, this ensured that U.S. forces would retain control of Kentucky for the rest of the war.

Yet that was not easy. Confederate forces held more than half of Kentucky until early 1862. While Lincoln's chief general at the moment, George B. McClellan, was struggling in the eastern theater of the war, entrenching on Virginia's James River after the miserable failure of his Peninsula Campaign and after Major General Ulysses S. Grant won victories over the Rebel forts on the Mississippi, Confederate major general Edmund Kirby Smith marched out of Knoxville, Tennessee, on August 14, 1862, intent on a new invasion of central Kentucky. Two weeks later, Confederate general Braxton Bragg left Chattanooga to join Kirby Smith in Kentucky. Union general Don Carlos Buell responded on August 30 by ordering units to pursue the Confederate invaders.

The little town of Munfordville, about seventy-four miles due south of Louisville and Pewee Valley, was the scene of four days of sharp combat as the forces clashed during September 14–17, 1862. It dragged out when the Confederates launched a premature assault on the town, which was repulsed with heavy losses on the first day of battle. As the Union reinforced the town, Braxton Bragg, as was his custom, became less strategic and more angry. He sent Simon Bolivar Buckner with a larger force, which had the Union position surrounded by the sixteenth. Buckner sent a formal demand for surrender.

Union colonel J.T. Wilder was an industrialist from Indiana and had absolutely no military training or experience. But he knew he had 4,133 men under his command, and he knew that the idea of surrender didn't appeal to him. Still, being a military newbie, he did not know what to do. So, he responded to Buckner's demand by calling on his headquarters under a flag of truce. He explained to the Confederate commander that he was ignorant of military matters, but he did know enough to be confident that, as an officer and a gentleman, Buckner would not deceive him with deliberately bad advice. So, he asked, pointblank, what he should do.

Somewhat at a loss, Buckner explained that it would be improper and ungentlemanly for him to advise his enemy on how to respond to a surrender demand. Wilder said that he understood but, pausing, asked if he might be permitted to inspect Buckner's forces so that he could count the cannon. Buckner agreed and led him on a tour of inspection. That completed, Wilder politely turned to the Confederate and said, "I believe I'll surrender."

Bizarre as it was, the fall of Munfordville cut Buell's communications with Louisville. Bragg must have known that this opportunity would not last long, but he chose not to exploit his advantage and decided to avoid further battle until he could unite forces with Kirby Smith. His immediate aim was to occupy Kentucky so that he could recruit sympathetic troops and establish supply depots before he launched into large-scale combat on the border between North and South.

It was a blunder. For at about this time, on September 19, Union general William S. Rosecrans, fighting under Grant, defeated some seventeen thousand Confederate troops under General Sterling Price at Iuka, Mississippi. Price retreated southward, and Confederate general Earl Van Dorn advanced to join forces with him. En route, believing that Corinth, Mississippi, was only lightly defended, Van Dorn attacked the town on October 3. To his chagrin, Iuka was held by twenty-three thousand troops under "Rosy" Rosecrans, which gave him a one-thousand-man advantage over Van Dorn. Grant immediately reinforced Rosecrans, adding to his superiority of numbers. On October 4, Van Dorn suffered a bloody repulse and retreated to Holly Springs. This cut off Bragg in Kentucky and denied him any hope of reinforcement. Taking advantage of the situation, General Buell maneuvered the now highly vulnerable Bragg into a major battle at Perryville, Kentucky, only a bit farther from Louisville and Pewee Valley, on October 8.

Buell had nearly thirty-seven thousand troops, whereas Bragg had no more than sixteen thousand available at Perryville. There was every reason to anticipate a glorious Union victory, but Buell proved unable to marshal his full forces. He did push Bragg and Kirby Smith out of Kentucky and into eastern Tennessee but failed to give pursuit. Having frittered away the opportunity for a decisive Union victory, Buell was replaced as commander of the Union's Department of the Ohio with Rosecrans. Nevertheless, by the middle of October, the Union had managed to beat back the Confederate invasion of Kentucky.

This did not mean that Kentucky was free from conflict. Confederate raiders also swept through the state. John Hunt Morgan, the fabled "Gray Ghost of the Confederacy," raided Kentucky three times. The so-called First Kentucky Raid began during the early morning of July 9, 1862, when he and his men crossed the Cumberland River from Tennessee and surprised the Union position in Tompkinsville, Kentucky, capturing the Union soldiers garrisoned there. From here, they advanced north through Kentucky, raiding Lebanon and Springfield before marching north to Bluegrass and then, moving southward, back across the Cumberland into Tennessee.

Months later, Morgan prepared to launch the so-called Christmas Raid of 1862. On December 23, with nearly four thousand men, Morgan crossed into Kentucky; camped in Tompkinsville; attacked and captured Glasgow, routing a small Union force; and then fought a pitched battle on Christmas Day at Bear Wallow, near Cave City. On December 28, Morgan captured six hundred Union troops guarding two trestles on Muldraugh Hill. He burned the bridges, which severed Union general William S. Rosecrans's rail supply line. Rosecrans caught up with him at the Rolling Fork River near Boston, between Elizabethtown to the southwest and Bardstown to the east.

The next summer, on July 2, 1863, Morgan crossed the Cumberland River into Kentucky at Burkesville and Neeley's ferries with 2,500 men. They skirmished with several Union units and continued raiding until they were hit hard at Tebbs Bend in an exchange that claimed 71 of Morgan's raiders. But Morgan pulled out of Kentucky and raided over great distances through Indiana and Ohio and West Virginia through the end of July, when, his numbers greatly reduced, Morgan and others were captured. On November 27, Morgan and 6 of his officers escaped from the penitentiary in which they had been held.

The last serious Confederate action in Kentucky came on March 25, 1864, when Confederate cavalry commander Nathan Bedford Forrest, fierce and brilliant, raided Paducah, a battle in which Forrest's 3,000 men overwhelmed 650 Union troops. Strategically, Forrest's victory meant little, but it showed Kentuckians that the Confederates could still penetrate deep into Kentucky. To the state's Unionists, this was demoralizing. To those

Kentuckians who favored the Confederacy, it gave hope to what many were already calling a Lost Cause.

Perhaps nothing encapsulates the divisions within Kentucky as much as the fact that both Abraham Lincoln and his wife, Mary Todd, were born in Kentucky, as was Jefferson Davis, president of the Confederate States of America. While much of the Civil War was fought close to the Eastern Seaboard, President Lincoln told his Illinois friend Orville Hickman Browning, "I think to lose Kentucky is nearly the same as to lose the whole game."[51]

Idyllic Pewee did not escape the war. Louisville began, like the state, as neutral in the war but, on February 21, 1861, hoisted an outsized American flag over the county courthouse. In 1860, the city's voters had overwhelmingly supported John Bell of Tennessee, a pro-slavery but pro-Union candidate, for president. Nevertheless, slavery was a diminishing institution in and around Louisville, the number of slaves in the city decreasing by 10 percent to 4,903, which was less than 10 percent of the Louisville population. Indeed, Irish immigrant labor offered strong competition to slave labor. Still, Louisvillians remained divided. Those who strongly supported the Union tended to read and rally around the *Louisville Daily Journal*, edited by George Prentice, while those who favored the Confederate cause read the *Louisville Morning Courier*, owned by Walter N. Haldeman.

The Confederate Editor

Born in Maysville, Kentucky, in 1821, Haldeman was sixteen when his family moved to Louisville. He bought his first paper in the city, the *Daily Dime*, in February 1844 and changed its name to the *Morning Courier* on June 1 of that year. Haldeman teamed with various business partners and editors over the years, including two, Edwin Bryant and William D. Gallagher, who would become his neighbors when, in the autumn of 1854, he moved from Louisville to Smith's Station, which had not yet been christened Pewee Valley. We met Bryant in chapter 4, an established journalist who had built a significant fortune with *What I Saw in California*, his guidebook to the 1848–49 gold rush. Gallagher was a poet by passion and a journalist by necessity who become the second editor of the *Morning Courier* until he parted ways with Haldeman over slavery. Haldeman was pro, Gallagher anti. Haldeman bought him out.

Walter Haldeman's 1854 move to Smith's Station was prompted by his wife, Elizabeth, who had absented herself from February to September

Walter Haldeman was one of Louisville's premier newspaper publishers—and an unabashed propagandist for the Confederacy. Sunnyside (later renamed Edgewood) was his summer palace—until the Union army seized it. After the Civil War, Haldeman became the founding father of Naples, Florida. *Pewee Valley Historical Society.*

of 1854 in Cleveland at the Cleveland Water Cure.[52] She was convinced that the noxious air of Louisville was killing her— and she may have been right. A city of many ponds, it was the breeding ground of such mosquito-borne diseases as malaria and yellow fever as well as the waterborne plagues typhus and cholera. The city earned the unenviable sobriquet of "Graveyard of the West." Smith's Station was both farther from the toxic Ohio River wetlands and considerably higher in elevation. At the time, you could get a charming and fashionable Victorian Italianate home (with a rural tin roof, mind you) on fifty acres in Smith's Station for $4,000, about $145,000 today. And it was already a very nice place to live, with plenty of interesting folks, including the local historian Ben Casseday; teacher, author, and spinner of myth Noble Butler; and novelist Catherine Anne Warfield.

Next door to Haldeman's property was a forty-acre estate developed by William H. Walker, who owned Walker's Exchange, Louisville's most distinctive combination gustatory emporium, saloon, and fine-dining restaurant. A *Louisville Courier* ad of the era billed it as "*Ne plus ultra*":

> *We are daily receiving per American Express Fresh Shell Oysters, Clams, Venison, Squirrels, Prairie Grouses, Bluewing Ducks, Quails, Plovers, Snipes, etc., including all the delicacies of the season, served up in our Restaurant and private apartments or sent to gentlemen's residences in superior style.*
>
> *Our Billiard Saloon has been neatly fixed up—new tables with Mike Phelan's patent cushions, to which we call the attention of our friends and the public.*[53]

As for the details of Walker's rural home, little is known other than what he named it: Vinona. It was destroyed by fire in December 1863 and never rebuilt. John Van Horne, a telegraph company executive, bought the acreage and built the Van Horne House on it in 1870.

Haldeman's 1854 house, which he named Sunnyside (the next owner renamed it Edgewood), befit a prosperous man and may even have made his ailing wife happy. His *Morning Courier* got behind non-abolitionist, noncommittal James Buchanan in the election of 1856 in an era when a *quid* could be counted on to earn a nice juicy *quo*, which in Haldeman's case was a plum federal patronage job as surveyor of customs for the port of Louisville. Haldeman turned over the paper to his hired editors and devoted himself to collecting the customs revenues on which his generous federal remuneration depended. In the 1860 election, the *Courier* endorsed Kentuckian Democrat John C. Breckinridge, whom the Republican Abraham Lincoln defeated. (The people of Louisville preferred John Bell of Tennessee, a pro-slavery but pro-Union candidate.)

The *Courier* took a stand against Lincoln's antislavery platform and stirred the secession pot, warning that a victorious Lincoln would possess the tremendous power of the federal government to "subjugate the south." Although Haldeman was not a plantation owner, he did own one slave, Elva, presumably his children's "mammy." But he used his paper less to extoll slavery than to preach the impossibility of stopping secession:

> *We have heard but one opinion of the inaugural* [Lincoln's 1861 inaugural address] *expressed and that opinion is, that it is a declaration of war....The address will be read with care and attention by the people of the border slaveholding states. It will teach them the hopelessness, the folly, the madness of trusting to the honor, to the love of justice or to the patriotism of the people of the Free states....Reconstruction of the federal union is now impossible. The slave states must and will unite in a common government and the Free states must and will form another confederacy.*[54]

After the attack on Fort Sumter on April 12, 1861, Haldeman rejected all news reports from the press pool northern papers used and instead hired his own Confederate-leaning correspondent, Charles D. Kirk, who referred to the Union forces simply as "the enemy." The U.S. government read Haldeman's paper and promptly snatched away his bread-and-butter customs post.

Although Haldeman lost his government job, Kentucky's neutrality protected both the *Courier* and Haldeman himself—at least until September 19, 1861, when the state legislature nullified the governor's neutrality policy by asking the Federal government for troops capable of expelling the Confederate "invaders." In the meantime, the U.S. Congress passed the Confiscation Act of 1861, authorizing Union troops to seize slaves and other property deemed to support the Rebel cause. Major General Robert Anderson, who had, at the outbreak of the war, commanded Fort Sumter and was now the Union commander in charge of defending Louisville, immediately invoked the Confiscation Act to ban the *Courier* from the mails. He sent a United States marshal to seize the paper's offices and to arrest its former editor Reuben Thomas Durrett, a prominent Confederate sympathizer. Haldeman evaded arrest, however, because he was holed up in Pewee Valley, some eighteen miles from *Courier* headquarters. However, a small group of Haldeman's friends (including Noble Butler and William Walker) took the train into Louisville to meet with General Anderson at the Louisville Hotel. They conveyed Haldeman's pledge to abstain from political commentary from now on and even allow the U.S. military to censor his paper—if he were only allowed to continue publishing.

The cold, hard fact was that, without his federal sinecure, he needed the *Courier* to keep generating revenue. He was deeply in debt. Anderson listened and agreed, stipulating, however, that Haldeman not only stop his pro-Confederate agitation but write and publish an article apologizing for his past actions and swearing fealty to both Kentucky and the Union. Haldeman bowed to the demand, and the required article appeared the next day. But when a messenger arrived at Sunnyside bearing a letter for Haldeman from the U.S. marshal authorizing the reopening of the newspaper, the recipient was not at home. He had made haste to Bowling Green, Kentucky, where Confederate general Simon Bolivar Buckner had his HQ.

Those who had vouched for him with General Anderson were appalled at having been betrayed. As for the Confederate "shadow government" based in Bowling Green, it named Haldeman its official printer. He now published the *Courier* as a Confederate newspaper, soon moving its offices to Nashville, Tennessee. Sunnyside was left behind, along with its occupants, Haldeman's wife, Elizabeth, and the couple's children. Haldeman had taken the precaution of transferring title to Sunnyside to Elizabeth, but that legal dodge failed to stop Union troops from seizing the property. In December 1861, Union military authorities gave her and her children a pass to cross Confederate lines and reunite with Walter Haldeman. Sunnyside and the Louisville-based *Courier* were seized and auctioned off to satisfy the owner's creditors.

The Nashville-based *Courier* served as a propaganda sheet for the Confederate government until the fall of Nashville to Union forces on February 16, 1862. With wife and children in tow, Haldeman fled successively to Chattanooga, Atlanta, and Knoxville. He ceased printing the *Courier* and went into the profitable whiskey distilling business until he was forced to flee again, late in the summer of 1863. The Haldemans lived as best they could first in Madison, Georgia, and then in Abbeville, South Carolina, where they waited out the war.

Walter Haldeman proved to be a survivor. He feared that he might be arrested when he returned to Louisville, but on the contrary, he was greeted as a hero. Union occupying forces had not treated Louisville well, and many Louisvillians had newfound sympathy for the Lost Cause of the Confederacy. Haldeman quickly raised $40,000 to restart the *Courier* and printed his first postwar issue on December 4, 1865. Within a year, the *Courier* was the city's most successful newspaper. In 1868, it merged with its pro-Union rival, the *Louisville Journal*, becoming the *Courier-Journal* with Haldeman as corporate president. The paper survives to this day, under the auspices of the Gannett chain.

Haldeman went on to become the founding father of Naples, Florida, and the owner of an early Major League Baseball team, the Louisville Grays. In May 1902, he was hit by a Louisville streetcar, developed peritonitis, and died on May 14, 1902, age eighty-one. The Haldemans had never returned to Pewee Valley.

THE KENTUCKY CONFEDERATE HOME

Smith's Station—or Pewee Valley—was, like Walter Newman Haldeman, a survivor. Louisville, which most Smith's Station residents considered their primary home, at times reaped considerable profit from the war. The city was a major supply depot, and fortunes were made supplying the needs of the Union army. Hotels and other public buildings were patronized by Union officers, to the great benefit of their owners.

Yet Louisville also lived in continual fear of attack by Confederate forces, and under a series of Union officers who held the title of commander of the Military District of Kentucky, the city suffered various indignities. On February 15, 1864, General Stephen Burbridge was named to that lofty post. A petty, vengeful, corrupt martinet, Burbridge earned the enmity of the city by refusing to issue trade permits to businessmen with known or suspected Confederate sympathies. He also freely interfered with the local electoral process, wheedled profitable patronage jobs for his political cronies, and arrested those he deemed enemies—either to himself personally or to the

Old and infirm Kentucky Confederate vets gather in the parlor of the Kentucky Confederate Home. *Kentucky Historical Society.*

United States—on the flimsiest of evidence. He was zealous in suppressing guerrilla activities with lynch-like "justice."

As the war petered out locally with the defeat of Confederate forces in the region, Louisville's economy deflated rapidly. Formerly prosperous shopkeepers were sometimes reduced to begging on the city's streets. In the aftermath of a Union victory toward which most Louisvillians had worked and for which they had hoped, the city's inhabitants turned from mostly pro-Union to totally disgusted with the federal government. By war's end, Louisville had become generally sympathetic to the Lost Cause of the Confederacy.

This did not carry over to Pewee Valley, which the shooting war had largely bypassed, as if the place had indeed been enchanted. The legacy of the war was a mixture of respectful remembrance and nostalgic healing.

Early in 1902, on the heels of a relentless lobbying effort by Kentucky ex-Confederate organizations, the state's General Assembly passed legislation to establish the Kentucky Confederate Home to care for aged, infirm, and impecunious Confederate veterans of the Civil War. The sponsoring veteran organizations were obliged to acquire an appropriate residential building on at least thirty acres, fully furnished and ready to care for at least twenty-five persons. The state would finance operations of the home. Newspapers across the state encouraged communities to consider hosting the home, which, they promised, would "serve as a constant source of revenue to the inhabitants of the lucky town."[55]

Pewee Valley, quite uninterested, declined to offer a bid. As the deadline for bid submission approached, Louisville businessman A.M. Sea met with Angus Neil Gordon, who owned the Villa Ridge Inn. It was an aging luxury hotel, now bankrupt, but sited on thirty-three choice acres near the Pewee Valley Train Depot. It had long since become a financial albatross, and Gordon was a highly motivated seller. The veterans' groups were persuaded to make an offer. The former hotel was a good fit. The veterans' groups had raised little money, but Gordon was willing to sell the hotel and its grounds to them for what little they had to offer. This was most welcome after other candidate towns—Owensboro, Hawesville, Glasgow, Bowling Green, Frankfort, Versailles, Nicholasville, Winchester, Bardstown, Franklin, and Harrodsburg—had properties on offer that either came too dear or had fatal flaws (tumbledown disrepair, a swampland site, or both).

Kate Matthews photographed Fannie Craig teaching the Gaines children at the Villa Ridge School, which occupied the ground floor of the Villa Ridge Inn. *Pewee Valley Historical Society.*

All these towns had one thing in common: they had vigorously sought to host the Home. At last, however, the choice came down to two: Harrodsburg and Pewee Valley. Like the other contenders, Harrodsburg really wanted the Home. Unlike the others, Pewee Valley never even put itself in the running. The Harrodsburg property was a landmark home that included outbuildings and had a price tag of $10,500, with the merchants of Harrodsburg promising to kick in $3,000 for furnishings and other improvements.

Villa Ridge Inn in Pewee Valley needed some repairs and sprucing up, but it was a sound structure and, even better, came fully and quite attractively furnished. It was also big. The hotel had seventy-two guest rooms, a dining hall and kitchen, running water, steam heat, and gas lighting. It offered easy access, by rail and by road, to nearby Louisville. Most of all, the price was right. Gordon asked for just $8,000 in cash plus a certain available Louisville property. The decision was obvious. Pewee Valley won.

The only problem was that no one in Pewee Valley wanted a Confederate Veterans Home. Judge Peter B. Muir, whom we met in chapter 4, living in octogenarian semi-retirement in his Pewee Valley home, told the *Courier-Journal* on September 5, 1902, one day after the deal was announced, that "the people don't want such a home here. The people of Pewee Valley believe that such an institution of the kind must hurt the place." With that, he swore he would fight it tooth and nail. Other prominent locals joined in his opposition. "Among the summer residents of Pewee Valley the feeling against the Home is undoubtedly strong," one newspaper observed. Pewee Valley was one of the "most fashionable suburbs about Louisville, and the people seem a bit discomfited by the advent of this public benevolent institution." As a Richmond, Kentucky newspaper editor wrote: "While a dozen other towns are tearing their hair out in their efforts to secure the Confederate Home, the citizens of Pewee Valley raise a terrible howl because they have gotten it."

The attitude was understandable, and winning hearts and minds would not be easy. The people of Pewee had to be made to understand that more than forty thousand Kentucky men had fought in the Confederate army. Most were able simply to return to their homes after the war, but some were afflicted with long-term disabilities and infirmities, the result of war wounds, and others were the victims of disease and old age. Because the state offered no institutional support and no pension and neither did the federal government, local families and organizations campaigned to demonstrate the need for a Confederate Home. Soon, the tide of public sentiment turned against Muir and the other objectors. As one newspaper editor scolded,

"There is too much aristocracy at Pewee Valley to permit poor and crippled Confederate veterans to be seen perambulating the place from day to day." In the end, the resistance simply ran out of air.

The Kentucky Veterans Home opened on October 23, 1902, in an atmosphere of celebration, and until 1934, it served more than seven hundred aged and ailing residents in a gracious old building on the crest of a gentle slope some few hundred yards from the Pewee Valley Depot. It was (as author Rusty Williams describes it) "four stories high, sixty feet deep and as long as seven rail cars. A wide veranda, furnished with comfortable rocking chairs and wooden gliders, surrounded the building on three sides, and it was said residents could enjoy a mile-long covered stroll. Second-story balconies and generous windows on every floor provided splendid views of area homes and churches as well as natural cross-ventilation. Atop the frame building was an octagonal cupola and, atop the cupola, eighty feet above neat flower beds, was a flagpole from which on this day flew the United States and Confederate flags."[56]

On the night of March 25, 1920, fire, the persistent demon of the valley's wooden structures, swept through the Confederate Home. "Rebel yells, resounding throughout the home, gave the alarm of fire," the *Courier-Journal* reported on March 26, "and all those able to walk, hurried from the building. By telephone, residents of Pewee Valley were asked for aid." Most of the "132 veterans at the home were members of [Brigadier General John Hunt] Morgan's Cavalry ["Morgan's Raiders"]." Of these residents, 59 were disabled or semi-disabled hospital patients. These men "were carried to safety in the church by residents of the little town, at the direction of Sergt. Gus Head, who, back in the days when 'Yanks' were the same to a Johnny Reb as a cactus thorn under a horse blanket, groomed General Morgan's gray stallion."[57]

Efforts to fight the blaze were hampered when a "big automobile pump" (pumper fire engine) ran into a ditch before it arrived on the scene. "For forty minutes, citizens of Pewee Valley tugged, until the fire engine was literally carried up an incline. It was then taken down another hill to a lake. It was too late to save the hospital and outbuildings, but Duke's Hall, which adjoined the hospital, was saved. Hundreds of persons, who went to the scene in every sort of conveyance, assisted the firemen in fighting the blaze." Even worse was the sudden explosion of an eighty-foot-high ten-thousand-gallon water tank from the fire's "intense heat," which meant that no water was available for twenty minutes.[58] By 1932, the population of what was left of the Kentucky Confederate Home had dwindled to eleven veterans. Two years later, on July 18, 1934, the five remaining "inmates" were transferred to Pewee Valley Hospital and Sanitorium, and the Confederate Home was no more.[59]

On April 28, 1937, the *Courier-Journal* reported on a proposal by Kentucky's governor to turn the abandoned Kentucky Confederate Home into a women's prison. Mr. and Mrs. Oscar Campbell, who were running the Sweet Shop at 301 LaGrange Road (see chapter 7), supported the proposal:

> *"The old Confederate Home is here and it has to be used in some way,"* asserted Mr. Campbell. *"Most of the people who are objecting are those who already have 'theirs,' but I notice they aren't making any move to buy the property."*
>
> *Mrs. Campbell added. "We're for it. During the flood when we had refugees here, we took in $10 more on a day at the shop and the prison would mean more than that."*
>
> *James Foley and B.P. Million, also storekeepers, said they had no objection to the proposal, but that they were not taking sides. "The property belongs to the State and if they want to put the prison here, it's up to them," said Foley. "We have a good State government and they'll do what's right."*[60]

What does remain to this day is the Confederate Burying Ground, 11,275 square feet deeded to the Commonwealth of Kentucky for use by the Kentucky Confederate Home. It is the final resting place of 313 Confederate veterans, most of them former residents of the Home. One of sixty-one Kentucky Civil War monuments in the National Register of Historic Places, it is the state's only official Confederate military cemetery.[61]

The Confederate Burying Ground is a picturesque Civil War memory within Pewee Valley, but by far the strongest surviving link to the war and its long aftermath is a work of children's fiction, the "Little Colonel" series of books. Immensely popular in the United States and even internationally through the mid-twentieth century, the books spun off dolls, diaries, board games, and even clothing, as well as *The Little Colonel*, a 1935 movie starring Shirley Temple and best remembered today for the iconic staircase dance Shirley does with the great Bill "Bojangles" Robinson. Resident Pewee author Annie Fellows Johnston based the setting and characters of the book (and the series of books that followed) on Pewee Valley. We have devoted all of chapter 8 to the "Little Colonel."

Chapter 6

INSIDE THE HISTORIC DISTRICTS

The United States really puts the "new" in the New World. In contrast, say, to Europe, where hundred-year-old buildings are considered reasonably modern and thousand-year-old buildings are not uncommon, a survey conducted by the U.S. Census in 2009 found the median age of American houses to be thirty-six years. A study by a Canadian forest services company—which included all sorts of structures, not just houses—found that of a sample of 227 buildings in North America that were condemned and demolished, most were less than fifty years old.[62]

Fortunately, since passage of the National Historic Preservation Act of 1966, the National Park Service has maintained a National Register of Historic Places, the official list of the nation's historic places deemed worthy of preservation. States, tribes, and other federal agencies, acting on information from the public, nominate historical properties that Americans want to protect. National Register personnel evaluate nominated buildings for their age, significance, and integrity. Those that earn listing in the Register are given special legal protection and, often, federal preservation grants and tax credits. While inclusion on the Register is national in scope, the process starts locally, with individuals interested in preserving the built heritage of their community.

Nobody would confuse Hoboken, New Jersey, located just across the Hudson River from Manhattan, with Pewee Valley, Kentucky, eighteen miles outside downtown Louisville. But what they have in common is a compact geographical size. Hoboken is 1.25 square miles in extent, and Pewee Valley consists of 1.93 square miles of dry land. But consider: Hoboken packs 57,703 people (2022 estimate) into its 1.25 square miles, while Pewee Valley distributes 1,618 folks (2022 estimate) across its 1.93. In terms of population density, that's a whopping 48,335 people per square mile for Hoboken versus just under 821 per square mile for Pewee Valley.

So what?

Here's what: thinly populated Pewee Valley claims thirty-five listings in the National Register of Historic Places while thickly populated Hoboken racks up just twenty-three. Moreover, while Pewee Valley was settled at the start of the nineteenth century and incorporated in 1870, the settlement of Hoboken, in a much older part of the nation, dates back to the seventeenth century. Very, very few places so recent in settlement and so small in population and geographical extent can claim as many historically significant structures as Pewee Valley.

Pewee Valley has two historic districts recognized in the National Register—the Central Avenue Historic District and the Ashwood Avenue Historic District—in addition to thirteen individual buildings outside of the districts.

Central Avenue Historic District[63]

Built in 1856 for Thomas and Nannette Smith, **Woodside** (at 110 Central Avenue) is one of the earliest antebellum homes that survive in the Central Avenue Historic District. An article in the *Louisville Democrat* (March 19, 1856) noted that this two-story Gothic Revival home was the very first house visible to passengers getting off the train at Smith's Station. The article describes Woodside Cottage as "embowered by the tall trees, through which the summer sun steals and falls in broken fragments on the emerald grass." It goes on to evoke the vision of "its white walls gleaming amid the dark green leaves," so that the observer "cannot help thinking it was one of the houses built by the fairies in olden times for their especial favorites."[64] In 1858, Woodside caught fire, "but through the strenuous exertions of the neighbors, the fire was extinguished before any great amount of damage was done."[65]

The Smiths married in 1819, and Thomas became a leading newspaper editor in Lexington, Kentucky. Woodside was likely purchased as the Smiths' retirement place. His neighbors included fellow Lexingtonian Elisha

Warfield, who had an interest in the Lexington and Ohio Railroad and owned property in Pewee Valley. An even nearer neighbor was the prominent Louisville newspaper publisher Walter Haldeman (1821–1902), who lived at Sunnyside (later renamed Edgewood) next door to Woodside. Edwin Bryant, a partner with Haldeman in the *Louisville Dime* newspaper, lived with the Smiths. The Smiths sold Woodside in 1865 or 1866 but continued to live in the house or somewhere else in Pewee Valley.

Sunnyside (114 Edgewood Way) was built by Walter Newman Haldeman in 1858 and, as related in chapter 5, was seized by Union forces in 1861 because Haldeman used his paper, the *Louisville Courier*, as a vehicle for Confederate propaganda. The two-story brick house is an exquisite example of the Italianate style that was prominent in Pewee Valley and elsewhere in Oldham County. In 1864, Sunnyside was sold at auction to Alexander (Aleck) Craig, a prosperous Louisville hat merchant. He renamed it **Edgewood** and built a schoolhouse in the backyard, where the Craigs' daughter, Fannie, taught. She became the inspiration for Annie Fellows Johnston's fictional schoolteacher Miss Allison in the "Little Colonel" books. Although

Edgewood (formerly Sunnyside), with Alice Craig (Gatchel) at ease against a tree in the foreground. *Pewee Valley Historical Society.*

Alexander Craig died in 1869, members of the Craig family occupied the house into the 1920s.

In 1987, developers were planning to demolish Edgewood to make way for a subdivision. They offered to give the house to anyone willing to move it, build a basement, buy a lot, and restore it. My wife, Donna, and I purchased the house for a dollar, and this gave free rein to her passion for collecting, interpreting, and preserving Pewee Valley history. In 1988, the house was moved a short distance from its original site, though on the original property.[66] Except for a new brick-faced concrete-block foundation, the move resulted in almost no structural changes to the house. The two chimneys and the original stone steps leading to the front and one of the back entrances were moved with it.

Today, the **Pewee Valley Presbyterian Church** (119 Central Avenue) stands as a Gothic Revival complex consisting of an 1867 stone church, 1860 chapel-manse-parish houses, and a 1954 stone and brick education building, all of which are tied together by a glassed-in connector. The church was formed in 1866 by Pewee Valley residents who worked with a committee from the Presbytery of Louisville. Annie Craig, wife of Alexander, was among the founding members of the church. Her father, Dr. Burr Hamilton McCown, preached the dedicatory sermon on November 21, 1867. From the start, the church was racially integrated: its first member, "Aunt" Clary Gordon, was a Black woman. Its most famous pastor was Dr. Peyton Harrison Hoge, who presided from 1907 to 1929 (see chapter 2).

The building is an outstanding example of the Gothic Revival style adapted to a small rural church. Its gable roof is tiled in slate that is patterned in different colors. Outside, tall lancet windows alternate with stepped-stone buttresses along the front and sides. The ceiling is supported by three trusses detailed with simple Gothic tracery, and a small stained-glass roundel is located above the entrance doors.

While its distinguished architecture is sufficient to make it memorable, the Pewee Valley Presbyterian Church earned even wider fame for its portrayal in Annie Fellows Johnston's "Little Colonel" books as "the little stone church with its ivy-covered belfry." The author became a member of the church after she moved to **The Beeches**, and to this day, a plaque marks her pew. Johnston turned numerous church members into "Little Colonel" characters: Judge Peter Brown Muir became fictional Judge Moore; Fannie Craig, Miss Allison; Annie Craig, Mrs. McIntyre; Mary Craig Lawton and her children became Manly, Frances, Katherine, and Louise; Kate Matthews

Photographer Kate Matthews (left hand reaching for the proffered cup) enjoys tea al fresco with her sisters. Presumably, this is a carefully staged selfie. *Pewee Valley Historical Society.*

was translated into the fictional Katherine Marks; and Louise Cleland, wife of Reverend T.H. Cleland, took on two roles in the books: Mrs. Bisbee and Mrs. Clelling.

James Foley House (212 Mount Mercy Drive) was likely built by H.M. Woodruff in the late 1870s and was purchased by James Foley about 1900. Three Foley brothers lived there with their two sisters until they deeded it to St. Aloysius Church in 1944. In the 1920s, the Foley House was remodeled, transforming it from a late Victorian frame farmhouse into a two-story stuccoed home, blending Classical and Mission details.

The **Woodruff-Foley Brothers General Store** (220 Mount Mercy) was built in 1880 and is Pewee Valley's oldest—most would say finest—historic commercial building. H.M. Woodruff built it as a general store, and for some years, the Foley brothers operated a meat market in the rear of the building. They purchased the entire building from Woodruff in 1903, changing its name to Foley Brothers General Store, and in 1915 built an addition. The building is still in use today as a veterinary office.

The original **Peace Farm** tract was twenty acres. Today, about twelve acres, including the surviving cottage (100 Peace Lane), two surviving outbuildings, and the ruins of several others are included in the historic district. The burned house was probably built in 1856 or 1857 by William Keely (1816–1876), who in 1849 designed Louisville's Cathedral of the Assumption. After his death in 1876, the property was sold to Kate Caldwell, wife of Louisville attorney Isaac Caldwell. The Caldwells' daughter, Mary C. Peace, inherited the property on her father's death. She and her family lived in the large house until it burned in about 1900.

The Peace Farm cottage is a single-story, two-room Victorian vernacular house with weatherboard siding, a gable-on-hip roof, and a full-width front porch, all built about 1880. Despite its modest proportions, the house is generously ornamented. The roof features wooden cresting, a central brick chimney, and, on three sides, shed-roofed vents with scallop-edged louvers. To the rear of the original structure is an addition from about 1900, which has a bay window on its northeast side. Inside, the two original rooms have grand fourteen-foot ceilings and are finished with beaded tongue-and-groove boards. Each room has a fireplace with an Eastlake-style mantel.

The Gables (121 Central Avenue) was built about 1895 by Maria Dillingham Bakewell, sister-in-law of John James Audubon. An eclectic one-and-a-half-story cottage, it stands out in Pewee Valley for its precocious use of a soon-to-be-popular Dutch Colonial Revival gambrel roofline. Like **The Beeches** (discussed next), The Gables became famous for its association

The Gables was built about 1895 by Maria Dillingham Bakewell, sister-in-law of famed ornithologist-artist John James Audubon. *Pewee Valley Historical Society.*

with "Little Colonel" author Annie Fellows Johnston, who purchased it in 1913 to use as a guest house and rental property. Local tradition has it that she wrote *Two Little Knights of Kentucky* here while staying with relatives in the late 1890s.

Built on a square plan, the house features a gambrel roof with three dormers across the front façade. The double front entry doors have above them a beautiful fanlight of rose-tinted glass inscribed *Parva sed apta*—"Small but sufficient." The variety of windows is eclectic in the extreme and includes an English Revival diamond, a large Queen Anne–style oriel, and a Colonial Revival Palladian fanlight.

The Beeches (125 Central Avenue) was home to "Little Colonel" author Annie Fellows Johnston from 1911 until her death in 1931, a fact that makes it one of the best known of Pewee Valley houses. It was built in 1902 for Mary Craig Lawton, widow of Henry Ware Lawton, a U.S. Army major general who fought in the Civil War, Apache Wars, and Spanish-American

Kate Matthews's grandniece Marjorie Cecelia Fletcher stands before the Beeches, home of "Little Colonel" author Annie Fellows Johnston. The photograph was printed as a postcard. *Pewee Valley Historical Society.*

War. He was the only American general officer killed (1899) during the Philippine-American War (1899–1902).

The two-and-one-half-story weatherboarded house is a magnificent example of the Colonial Revival in American domestic architecture. The interior is graced by a large central hall with a classically detailed staircase and fireplace. The floors are parquet throughout the first floor. The Beeches is set back from the road on generous grounds that feature informal landscaping with shade trees and flowering trees and shrubs. Historic stone gate posts, a Pewee Valley landmark, mark the driveway, which loops around to the southeast side of the house.

With twenty-two rooms, two-story **Bemersyde** (14 Central Avenue) qualifies as a mansion. It is an eclectic structure in which Colonial Revival influences nevertheless predominate. The house was extensively remodeled in 1907 from a much smaller structure that had been built between 1880 and 1900. It is distinguished by a double-hipped roof and tall interior end

At twenty-two rooms in two stories, Bemersyde is one of the few historical Pewee Valley homes that qualifies as a genuine mansion. Reverend Peyton Harrison Hoge (Pewee Valley Presbyterian Church) and his wife purchased the home in 1907. *Pewee Valley Historical Society.*

chimneys. The glorious porch, with Tuscan columns and a solid frieze, wraps around the front and southeast sides of the house, bowing outward at the main entrance, which features double doors surmounted by a large transom. Earlier conical turrets over the corner extensions were (perhaps unfortunately) removed some time after 1907.

The site of Bemersyde was originally part of the **Woodside** tract until Reverend Peyton Hoge and his wife purchased the property in 1907 and commissioned the expansion not only to accommodate themselves and their six children but also the frequent entertaining incumbent upon a prominent Presbyterian clergyman. Hoge had been minister of Warren Memorial Presbyterian Church in Louisville and was chairman of the Building Committee for the Presbyterian Theological Seminary of Kentucky. He served as pastor and pastor emeritus of Pewee Valley Presbyterian Church from 1907 to 1929 (see chapter 2).

Pewee Valley State Bank (218 Mount Mercy Drive) was built in 1910. Handsome though diminutive, it is a single-story Neoclassical building, a gem among Pewee Valley's modest collection of historic commercial structures. Constructed of rock-faced concrete block, the bank sports a pedimented portico supported by pairs of Tuscan columns dominating the front façade. The central entrance consists of double glass doors below a large transom. The bank began doing business from this building on September 1, 1910, and in 1948 became a branch of the Bank of Oldham County, continuing to operate out of this building until 1963. In that year, the Pewee Valley Woman's Club bought the structure and owns it to this day.

For the many years that the bank operated independently, James J. Foley served as a director and president. He lived on one side of the bank, and Foley Brothers General Store was on the other side.

Pewee Valley's second general store, **W.N. Jurey's General Store** (300 Mount Mercy Drive), was built in 1912 by William Nice Jurey, who was not only the storekeeper but also the railroad depot agent. Over the years, the building came to house three grocery stores, the Pewee Valley Masonic Lodge, the main telephone exchange, the Pewee Valley Post Office, and, finally, the Little Colonel Playhouse. The two-story concrete-block building has a gable roof with a stepped parapet front on which a high-relief Masonic emblem is prominent. Jurey built the structure to replace his earlier Queen Anne–style store, which had been destroyed by fire earlier in the year.

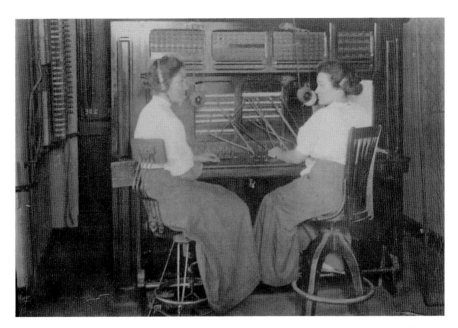

The second floor of W.N. Jurey's General Store housed a Masonic Lodge and the offices of the local telephone exchange, whose operators were doubtless kept busy with important calls from wealthy people.

The first floor of the building functioned as a store—under several different owners—until about 1960. Both the Masons and the local telephone exchange occupied space on the second floor. In 1969, the Little Colonel Players bought the entire building and have been staging productions there ever since.[67]

Built in 1923, the **Genevieve and Alfred Chescheir House** (120 Peace Lane) is the only Neoclassical brick residence in Pewee Valley. It is also one of the few large houses built here during the 1920s. The rectangular-plan structure is a five-bay, gable-roofed, brick-veneer house with an exterior end chimney. The front façade is dominated by its two-story pedimented portico supported on Ionic columns. Double-paneled doors are flanked by sidelights and topped with an oversized elliptical fanlight. The southeast side patio is original. The northwest side is a 1950s addition, with a bath and bedroom. The house sits among large pines, cedars, and shade trees on land that was part of the adjoining family estate. It was gifted to Genevieve by her mother, Gertrude A. Ross.

Like the Genevieve and Alfred Chescheir House, **Twigmore** (121 Peace Lane), was built in 1923. Architecturally, it is of even greater distinction than the Chescheir House across the street. Indeed, it is the only documented architect-designed house in all of Pewee Valley. Built of local limestone in the English Revival style, Twigmore was designed by Charles Marcus Osborne of the nationally renowned Boston architectural firm of Cram and Ferguson. Osborne was the cousin of the owner, Lillian Fletcher, and designed the house in emulation of the English Cotswold cottages Fletcher admired. A local stonemason, Charlie Miller, built the house, and Alfonse Singer, another Pewee local, did all the millwork and carpentry.

Set back from the road on a lightly wooded lot landscaped with a heavy ivy ground cover, Twigmore is accessed by a meandering path leading from a beautiful cast-iron gate on the Central Avenue entrance. A distinctive "Pewee Valley–style" wooden fence runs along the property's Central Avenue frontage, and a row of osage orange trees marks the rear property line.

Lillian Fletcher came to Pewee Valley as a young woman to live with her relatives, the Edward Matthewses; photographer Kate Matthews was Lillian's

Above: Exuberantly overgrown, this was Twigmore in 1935. *Pewee Valley Historical Society.*

Opposite: Lillian Fletcher was mistress of Twigmore, whose design she commissioned from society architect Charles Marcus Osborne, her cousin. Her name after she married Hollywood writer/producer (*Ninotchka, The King and I, Lost Weekend, Sunset Boulevard,* and more) Charles Brackett was Lillian Fletcher Brackett. *Pewee Valley Historical Society.*

aunt. After the death of her sister, Lillian married her former brother-in-law, screenwriter and producer Charles Brackett, who wrote and/or produced some forty films, among them such iconic movies as *Ninotchka, The King and I, Lost Weekend,* and *Sunset Boulevard.* Lillian Fletcher Brackett lived with her husband in Hollywood but retained her Pewee Valley house, returning to live there in 1969, after Brackett's death.

Ashwood Avenue Historic District[68]

The Ashwood Avenue Historic District is smaller than the Central Avenue Historic District but is especially distinctive. Except for one house from 1936, the structures listed in the district were built between 1890 and 1911, the era in which Pewee Valley was at its most glamorous.

The **Truman-Nock House** (116 Ash Avenue) was built about 1890 by Harry C. Truman to replace a house that had burned. An officer (cashier) of the Kentucky National Bank in Louisville, he married, in September 1881, Hattie Semple, the daughter of A.C. Semple, a prominent Louisville businessman. Truman sold the house in 1897 to attorney Robert Nock and his wife, Annie. The Nock family lived in the house well into the 1930s.

The two-story structure is one of very few Queen Anne–style homes in Pewee Valley. The gable roof is shallow pitched, with an oversized dormer at

The Truman-Nock House was built in 1890 by bank officer Harry C. Truman. He sold the house in 1897 to attorney Robert Nock and his wife, Annie. *Pewee Valley Historical Society.*

the front. The front porch spans the full width of the house, and a polygonal corner turret rises from a limestone block on the first floor. Sheathed in decorative shingles on the second floor, it is topped with a tent roof. Inside the house is a fine stair hall with sumptuous oak paneling and a spindle-work screen along the stairs. Large shade and pine trees have been allowed to partially hide the front of the house.

The **Washburne-Waterfill House** (100 Ash Avenue) was built about 1900 by George R. Washburne, a wealthy Louisvillian. It is believed to incorporate parts of an earlier home, built about 1870 at this location. Although Washburne built the 1900 structure as a summer home, Joseph H. Waterfill, vice president of a Louisville bank, lived here with his family year-round after he purchased it from Washburne in 1910. The Waterfill family owned the house until 1942.

Built on an asymmetrical plan, the simplified Queen Anne style of the house also embraces features of the Craftsman Bungalow style. The roof is double-hipped, and the house is one and a half stories at the front and west sides, rising to two stories at the east and rear. The front porch, which is trimmed with short Tuscan columns on fieldstone piers, spans the entire width of the house and extends west, forming a porte-cochere. Historic stone gate posts mark entrances on LaGrange Road and at the corner of Ash Avenue. The property includes a carriage house (from about 1900) with board-and-batten siding and double gable roof and a servant's cottage with tar paper and batten siding (also from about 1900).

The **Washburne-Swann House** (106 Ash Avenue) was built about 1905 in the Victorian vernacular style on a modified T-plan with a cross-gable roof. A hip-roofed front porch is supported by simple square posts on limestone piers. A balustrade caps the porch roof and serves as the railing for a small front balcony. A nonhistoric single-story wing was at some point added at the rear of the east side. The use of vinyl siding may detract from the house but does not essentially alter its historic character.

It is believed that George Washburne built the house on spec about 1905. It was sold to the Harry R. Swann Jr. family in 1910.

The **Sherman and Cora Jurey Weatherlv House** (111 Ash Avenue) was built by the Weatherlys about 1905. It is a large two-and-one-half-story house in the Colonial Revival style and features a gable roof with a pedimented cross-gable that is balanced by a gable-roofed dormer on the front façade. A flat-roofed front porch spans the width of the house and was screened in at an unknown date. Its posts are not originals, but replacements. Attractive features include pedimented dormers and ends as well as a dentil frieze that runs around the house just under the cornice.

The front façade of what was originally a weatherboarded house was sided with aluminum at some point. The siding and the nonhistorical screened-in porch notwithstanding, the house retains much of its elaborately detailed historic character. The interior is especially fine, with its Mission-style mantel—complete with built-in clock! The dining room boasts built-in side cupboards.

From 1876 to the late 1890s, this property was the site of the Kentucky College for Young Ladies, which burned on August 28, 1900 (chapter 3). The Weatherlys, Sherman and Cora Jurey, were the original owners. Weatherly was employed by the Louisville and Nashville Railroad in Louisville. In the 1940s, the property was developed as a chicken farm.

Another 1905 house, at **115 Ash Avenue**, is almost identical to its 111 Ash Avenue next-door neighbor, the Sherman Weatherly House. Number 115 Ash, however, retains its original porch detailing, including truncated Corinthian columns on battered stone plinths, a frieze with a band of dentils, and a rooftop balustrade. At the time of the Historic Register application, the house had vinyl siding, which did not seriously degrade the historic character of the house. The 115 Ash Avenue house changed owners several times, making it impossible to determine the original owner.

The **Carrie D. Coleman House** (112 Ash Avenue) is believed to have been built in 1911 as a summer house to replace an earlier house destroyed by fire. It is a large one-and-one-half-story Craftsman Bungalow and is among the best examples in Pewee Valley of this very popular, very important style. The shallow-pitched gable roof is supported on rafters with trimmed ends and large eave brackets on the gable ends. The front porch, which spans the full width of the house, is recessed and supported by Tuscan columns. The railing is a modern replacement. Like several other notable houses in this historic district, the Coleman House has been sided with vinyl.

The **Mary Cleland House** (117 Ash Avenue) was built in 1915 by Mary (familiarly called Mamie) Cleland, whose father was a minister at Pewee Valley Presbyterian Church. She built the house for herself, her mother, and her brother. It is a two-story Craftsman-style structure, whose historical

Above: The house at 115 Ash Avenue changed owners so often that the identity of the original owners has been lost in the shuffle. Its historical value lies in its having retained so much of its original ornamental detailing. *Pewee Valley Historical Society.*

Right: Mary—better known in Pewee Valley as Mamie—Cleland pauses in her canter down Ashwood Avenue. The photograph is from the 1890s. *Pewee Valley Historical Society.*

character is somewhat compromised by the enclosure of the front porch and the addition of aluminum siding.

Built on a square plan, the house has a gable roof with a broad overhang and gable end brackets. The large porch wraps around the west corner of the house, but its original stone piers have been infilled with a low brick well and metal-frame windows. The house rests on a limestone block foundation, and a large single-story addition is located at the rear of the house. The entire Cleland house is nearly hidden from the road by large holly trees.

The **Charles Hoffman House** (121 Ash Avenue) is unique in Pewee Valley as its sole example of an American Foursquare house, a style that was popular elsewhere in the country from roughly the mid-1890s to the late 1930s. Charles Hoffman, a German American printer who worked for a German-language newspaper in Louisville, built the house about 1916.

The Charles Hoffman House, built about 1916, is unique in Pewee Valley as the village's only example of the American Foursquare house, a style popular throughout most of the nation from the late nineteenth century through the 1930s. *Pewee Valley Historical Society.*

Hoffman House has a high hipped roof with hipped dormers on three of its sides. The gable-roofed front porch spans three-quarters of the width of the house, is supported on Tuscan columns, and is surmounted by a pedimented gable. The foundation is local limestone block. A one-story addition extends to the rear of the house.

The newest house in the Ashwood Avenue Historic District, the **William Logsdon House** (110 Ash Avenue), was built in 1936 by the Logsdon family to replace their earlier dwelling on this site that was destroyed by the valley's all too familiar nemesis, fire. While the property is included within the historic district, the National Register application designates it as "NC" (non-conforming) because its original English Cottage style has been "seriously altered." The one-and-one-half-story house is built on a T-plan and has a gable roof with a projecting central front gable wing. The front façade has a large rustic brick exterior chimney, which is trimmed with stone. The front door of the house is arched and set in the brick.

Added at some point to the house were a large wraparound porch and a massive two-story rear wing. These additions tripled the size of the house, further altering its historic character significantly.

Chapter 7

OUTSIDE THE HISTORIC DISTRICTS

S ome of Pewee Valley's most intriguing and significant buildings and places are outside the town's two historic districts.

The **William A. Smith House**, also known as **Olde Pine Tower** (108 Mount Mercy Drive),[69] was built about 1860 by Henry S. Smith's son William Alexander Smith (1831–1909). It is one of the few surviving intact properties associated with the family of Henry Smith, the prime mover of Pewee Valley's early development.

William (1831–1900) was the second of three children born to Henry and Susan Smith. At the time of the 1850 census, all three children were living with their parents in Rollington. Papa Henry was listed in the census as a "mechanic," a word that, in the mid-nineteenth century, applied to any skilled or even semi-skilled manual laborer. His sons were listed as "laborers." Presumably, they worked for their father. First to marry was William, who wed Mary Ann Compton on October 9, 1851, in a ceremony performed by Samuel Helm, a "minister of the gospel of the church of christ [*sic*]." They would have eight children together and, so, were in need of a substantial house.

William Alexander Smith built his home on eight acres purchased from his father the year he was married. He was a builder by trade. It is assumed that he built the house himself, and Pewee Valley lore credits him with building other houses in the area as well. If he did indeed personally build his own house, he showed considerable mastery in executing a two-story Italianate house with some eclectic Stick-style elements. As it stands today, it even retains some of its historic landscaping. Henry Smith was an avid amateur horticulturalist, and William clearly took after him, planting a wide variety of trees on the property. He also grew grapes, as did many nineteenth-century residents of Pewee Valley.

By the 1870 census, the family was living in this home, with William's vocation now listed as "blacksmith," with his oldest son, William H., assisting him in the shop. By the 1880 census, we know that William Alexander was employed as a wagonmaker and five of his eight children still lived at home.

William Alexander Smith sold his house to the O'Neals and downsized to a much smaller dwelling next door. According to the census of 1900, he was working as a carpenter and living in the smaller home with his wife and daughter Susie, who never married.

In 1897, WILLIAM A. Smith designed Pewee Valley's town hall, and in 1905, son William H. Smith designed and built **The Sweet Shop** (301 LaGrange Road). It was originally built for his son-in-law Tom McAllister, who planned to rent it out to local businesses. Many businesses were housed in the building, but the longest lived was The Sweet Shop, which had several owners over the years. In 1910, the second floor was remodeled for use by the Pewee Valley Masonic Lodge, which had been formed that year. Two years later, in 1912, the Masons moved into the second floor of W.N. Jurey's general store.

Although there are scant records concerning the identity of The Sweet Shop tenants over the years, the store did suffer a bout with Pewee Valley's familiar nemesis, fire. On November 26, 1928, the *Courier-Journal* reported on the good work of telephone operators in saving the building:

> *Loss estimated at $6,000 was caused at 9:20 o'clock Sunday morning in Pewee Valley when fire, thought to have been caused by a defective flue, destroyed the two-story frame building in which the shop is located. G. Barber Head, proprietor of the shop, said his damages would amount to approximately $600. James Foley owned the building.*
>
> *Mrs. A.L. Herdt and Mrs. Mary Purvis, Pewee Valley telephone operators, called the Anchorage fire department for help, which was said to have saved the building from burning to the ground. The entire upper story was practically burned out and the first floor was damaged by water. Peter Miller, Jr., clerk at the store, was on duty at the time the fire broke out. Edward Baumeister, town marshal, and Peter Wilhoit turned in the alarm.*[70]

The *Courier-Journal* failed to note that Mrs. A.L. Herdt had called in the fire that struck the W.N. Jurey General Store back in 1912. Mrs. Herdt, who was then Miss Ida Ochsner, was working out of the telephone exchange office on the second floor of the store. After calling in the blaze, she had to climb down the telephone pole next to the store to escape the flames.[71]

Not everything that transpired at The Sweet Shop was heroic. The *Courier-Journal* of May 20, 1936, reported:

3 Hurt in Fight at Pewee Valley
Row Believed Started to Distract Attention; $10 Taken from Cash Register

Two men and a woman were injured and $10 was stolen from a cash register and peanut vending machine during a fight at 7:30 p.m. Tuesday in Horace Roney's Sweet Shop in Pewee Valley.

The injured, all of Pewee Valley, were S.F. Warren, 33, who received a broken jaw when he was struck with a beer bottle; Peter Wilhoyte, 26, cut in the face by a thrown glass; and Mrs. May Rhoederer, cut on the hand when she was knocked to the floor.

These three, Roney told the police, were in the shop when a group of five men and a woman entered, sat at a table and ordered beer. Directly, one of the men arose, walked to where Warren was sitting and without warning, struck him in the face with a bottle.

County police were of the opinion the fight was started to distract Roney's attention while one of the group rifled the cash drawer. The offensive group left the shop and drove away in an automobile that had been parked in front. A pursuit by Roney and others was unsuccessful. The injured were treated by Dr. John R. Peters at the Pewee Valley Hospital.[72]

St. James Episcopal Church (401 LaGrange Road) was built in 1869, and the site includes a rectory from 1911 and education building from 1965. The church, built from local limestone, is a single-story structure in the rural Gothic Revival style with a square tower that has a bellcast steeple. Clear glass (much of it original) set in pointed-arch windows alternates with stone buttresses on the side walls of the church. Set into the northwest gable façade is a rose window made of stenciled colored glass, and the altar bay has three pointed-arch windows with stenciled glass as well. The church's oak pews are original to the building.

The original plans for the church were created by one B. Talbott but completed by William H. Redin, an architect who had designed other rural

A deft sketch
of St. James
Episcopal Church
by Mary Johnston.
*Pewee Valley
Historical Society.*

Gothic Revival churches, including one, Anchorage Presbyterian Church, in nearby Jefferson County, which was listed in 1980 in the National Register. Redin lived for several years in Pewee Valley and is buried in the local cemetery.[73]

Built in 1914, **St. Aloysius Church** (201 Mount Mercy Drive) has its origin in the work of mission priests from the Cathedral of Louisville. They ministered to the local Pewee Valley congregation until 1863, when land was purchased for a small cemetery, Catholic Hill, which also accommodated the building of a small gabled church that was dedicated to St. Aloysius in 1865. Its congregation was served as a mission by priests from Shelbyville and from

Electric ("traction") interurban rail transportation supplemented steam locomotives in connecting Pewee Valley with Louisville. The Louisville and Eastern Railroad reached LaGrange, northwest of Pewee Valley, in 1907 but soon went bankrupt laying new track in the difficult Kentucky hill country. This photo likely dates from shortly before or after 1907. *Pewee Valley Historical Society.*

St. Aloysius Catholic Church was completed in 1914. *Pewee Valley Historical Society.*

the Cathedral of Louisville. In 1871, the year after the incorporation of Pewee Valley, a parish was established, which, in turn, provided missionary services to nearby communities.

In 1904, additional land was purchased on Mount Mercy Drive, which was called Railroad Avenue at the time and was adjacent to an interurban rail line running from LaGrange to Louisville. Construction started on a rectory in 1911, and in June 1913, the foundation for the new church was laid out and then dedicated by the Right Reverend Bishop O'Donaghue. The building was completed in June of the following year, 1914, and blessed on June 21, with Bishop O'Donaghue presiding.

Interestingly, it was long believed that the original 1869 church was demolished or burned down. Research conducted for the 125th anniversary of St. Aloysius revealed that it was actually purchased and moved across Rollington Road, where it became a private residence. The rectory from the original church grounds may have also been sold and repurposed as a private residence on Central Avenue—though there is some evidence that this building was actually St. Aloysius Hall.

In 1926, the Sisters of Mercy arrived at St. Aloysius and moved into a house west of the church, which had been deeded to the parish by Jeremiah Bacon, founder of Bacon's Department Store.[74]

Dr. Thomas C. Peebles House (114 Maple Avenue) was built about 1870 and is also known as **Stitchhaven**. It is a wood-frame Italianate structure on a two-and-one-half-acre landscaped property. The house is a two-story structure on an L-shaped plan. Sided in weatherboard, it has a shallow-pitched gable roof with a wide overhang and large brackets along the eaves. Paneled double doors flanked by narrow sidelights and topped by a narrow overlight form the front entrance. Inside are six original rooms, three on the main floor and three on the second floor. They are organized around a central stairway, which is highlighted by a very fine newel post. The first-floor windows and doorframes have elaborate shouldered surrounds. Four of the rooms retain original marble mantels with arched openings and central cartouches. The hardwood floors and paneled wainscoting in the parlor and stair hall were added in the 1940s, as was the Colonial Revival mantel in the parlor.

Rosswoods: The Van Horne–Ross House (138 Rosswoods Drive) was built about 1870 in the Italianate style that was highly popular in Pewee Valley. Originally, the house stood on forty acres at the intersection of Central

Avenue and Peace Lane. In 1978, the property around it was developed as the Ross Woods subdivision, but the house remains on its original location. The application for the Historic Register listing notes:

> *The Van Horne–Ross House occupies a small portion of what was originally a forty-acre property first developed in 1856 by William H. Walker, a Louisville businessman. Walker's house burned in 1863. Between 1866, when Walker sold the land, and 1870, when John D. Van Horne bought it, the property changed hands at least three times. It is presumed that Van Horne built the present house, although possibly one of the interim owners, Jonas H. Rhorer and Charles B. Cotton, both Pewee Valley land speculators, or Dr. J.E. Helm was responsible.*

From 1834 until into the 1890s, William H. Walker was a prominent presence in Louisville's food and beverage industry. In 1834, he opened the city's first tavern off Main Street, and it soon became the informal headquarters of Louisville's Whig Party. By 1845, the tavern had transitioned to fine dining and was renamed Walker's Restaurant Hotel. In 1851, it moved to a new building on Third Street, between Main and Market, becoming Walker's Exchange, offering the likes of "Fresh Shell Oysters, Clams, Venison, Squirrels, Prairie Grouses, Bluewing Ducks, Quails, Plovers, Snipes, etc., including all the delicacies of the season, served up in our Restaurant and private apartments or sent to gentlemen's residences in superior style."[75]

The house Walker built in 1856 was named Vinona, and in 1863 it met a fate all too common in Pewee Valley. As the *Daily Democrat* reported on December 19, 1863:

> **Destructive Fire in Pewee Valley.** *Between 1 and 2 o'clock yesterday morning, the fine residence of W.H. Walker, situated in Pewee Valley, caught fire, and, owing to a high wind which was prevailing at the time, the flames spread with such rapidity that in a short time the entire mansion, which was frame, was wrapped in one sheet of flames, and the family barely had time to escape with their lives. The house with its entire contents was destroyed in almost less time than it takes to relate it. All the furniture, fine paintings, books, clothing, and long-cherished mementoes of friendship and affection were utterly destroyed, nothing being saved from the burning building but a secretary containing private business papers. We did not learn Mr. Walker's exact loss, but understand that the property is*

partially insured in the Farmers' Mutual Insurance Company of this city. We learn that Mr. Walker intends in the spring to erect a fine stone mansion in the place of the one just destroyed.[76]

Walker never did build the "fine stone mansion" mentioned in the *Daily Democrat*, and in 1870, John Van Horne purchased the estate and the frame two-story house today known as the Van Horne–Ross House.

John Van Horne was general superintendent of the Southern Division—and later vice president—of the Western Union Telegraph Company. He was born in Centreville, New Jersey, in 1827 and became an apprentice telegrapher in 1850 in Buffalo, New York. He rose through the managerial ranks as an operator and a builder in Ashtabula, Milan, Massillon, Akron, and Sandusky, Ohio. After assignments elsewhere, he became general superintendent of the South-western Telegraph Company, headquartered in Nashville, Tennessee. With the outbreak of the Civil War, he was tasked with dividing the property of the company between North and South and became president of Western Union operations within Confederate lines.

After Van Horne's loyalty and talent prompted his elevation to the vice presidency of Western Union, he commuted by train to and from his office

Rosswoods, which is also known as the Van Horne–Ross House, was built in 1870 on forty acres. The house still stands, albeit surrounded by the Ross Woods subdivision. *Pewee Valley Historical Society.*

in Louisville and also served on the City of Pewee Valley's Board of Trustees for several years. On August 11, 1895, the *Courier-Journal* profiled the Van Horne home:

One of the most interesting dwellers in Pewee Valley is Mrs. Van Horn [sic], who has been living there for twenty-five years. The house is commodious, well-arranged and is surrounded by extensive and picturesque grounds. There are forty acres to the tract. The approach to the house is laid out in flower beds, and the long avenue is shaded by a number of grand old forest trees. The Van Horns have done much to establish the reputation of Pewee Valley for refinement. Mrs. Van Horn has a striking personality.

Some years ago, Mrs. Van Horn's family consisted of four young women, all of whom were talented musicians. Of them was Mrs. Cushman Quarrier, the favorite vocalist. As many as thirty young folks were daily visitors at the Van Horn home during the summer.

The place was formerly the property of Dr. Walker, a patent medicine man, who cultivated acres of the herb he used in the decoction of his bitters. Mrs. Van Horn usually has some of her family with her. The place was bought by her husband on the advice of his physicians, who prescribed fresh

Genevieve Ross married Alfred Smith Cheschier in 1907 and moved just next door into what is now known as the Ross-Cheschier House. *Pewee Valley Historical Society.*

air as necessary for good health. They had just gotten located when he was called to New York, where for twenty years he has been Vice President of the Western Union Telegraph Company. Mrs. Van Horn delights to speak of Pewee Valley and the happy days that she has spent here.[77]

After retiring from Western Union around 1897, Van Horne remained in his Pewee Valley residence. He died in December 1902, and in 1903, the Van Horne House was sold to the William Ross family. They bought it as a summer home but soon moved in permanently. William Ross (May 6, 1859–December 11, 1922) founded the Ross Seed Company in Louisville in 1895. Four years later, on February 27, 1889, he married Gertrude Doherty. The couple had four children, including Genevieve Ross Cheschier (December 3, 1889–November 8, 1975), who married Alfred Smith Cheschier in 1907 and moved into a home next to her parents' estate, now called the Ross-Cheschier House in Pewee Valley.

AFTER HE DIVORCED HIS wife, Gertrude, William Ross retired from his company and, in 1916, moved to San Diego, California. The 1920 census has him living on West Point Loma Linda Boulevard with his thirty-two-year-old married niece, Bettie Jane Milby. He died there on December 11, 1922. His son Charles commissioned an extraordinary monument for the Ross family, as reported in the *Middlesboro (Kentucky) Daily News* on March 15, 1923:

EGYPTIAN TOMB TO BE BUILT IN LOUISVILLE
A massive Egyptian tomb, patterned after that of…Tutankhamen, which was opened recently at Luxor, is to be built by a Louisville firm for the family of William Ross, founder of Ross Seed Company. An order for the tomb has been placed by Charles D. Ross, Louisville capitalist, as a memorial to his father.
More than a year will be required for construction of the tomb, on which work will begin around May 1. Data necessary for an accurate design is being obtained from Egypt, according to an official of the company which was awarded the contract.[78]

The "tomb" is located in Calvary Cemetery, Louisville, where William Ross was interred on October 30, 1923.[79]

Tanglewood (417 LaGrange Road) was built in 1869 as a wood-framed house in a blend of the Gothic Revival and Italianate styles. Built on an L-shaped plan, the house is one and a half stories with a three-story rectangular tower at the center front of the house in the angle of the *L*. The roof is a cross gable with a front gable-roofed dormer. A flat-roofed porch wraps around part of the front and north sides. The interior is laid out in a center-hall plan with four main rooms on each floor. The house was divided into three apartments during the 1940s but was subsequently restored to a single-family dwelling. The house sits on sixteen acres and has a roughly seven-hundred-foot frontage on LaGrange Road. It is bounded contiguously with the property of St. James Episcopal Church.

Tanglewood was built, on speculation, during a post–Civil War building boom that swept Pewee Valley. Louisa Dickson, wife of John F. Dickson, purchased it in February 1869 and sold it to Jonas H. Rhorer and Charles B. Cotton, two Pewee Valley residents who were heavily involved in real estate during the late 1860s and 1870s. Rhorer had ample funds to finance his real estate investments, but on January 9, 1880, he confessed to having embezzled from the Savings Bank of Louisville. It is not known whether his partner, Charles Cotton, was in on the larceny or even had any knowledge of it, but their Pewee Valley real estate empire enterprise instantly dissolved. Tanglewood was among the properties liquidated following Rhorer's conviction and bankruptcy. Before all this, Tanglewood had been rented or perhaps even owned by a Mr. Staltz, a fact that is known by its having been mentioned in a December 25, 1871 article in the *Courier-Journal*: "Country Seats. A Pen Picture of Pewee Valley." It is described in the piece as "the Swiss chalet of Mr. Staltz." The writer did view it from a distance—the platform of the Pewee Valley train depot—so perhaps, with its rising tower, it did call to mind a chalet. Or perhaps the writer had never visited Switzerland.[80]

After the liquidation of Rhorer's properties, the next Tanglewood purchaser was a J.H. Turner, in 1884. The Turner family owned the estate until 1911, when it was purchased for about $15,000 by attorney Aaron Kohn, at which point the estate consisted of "twenty-six acres of rich farmland and many improvements." After Kohn sold it, it passed through a number of owners until it was purchased by Mr. and Mrs. Grove Gleason in 1951. For years after that, the Gleasons raised donkeys and miniature horses on the property, and the animals became a familiar sight to those driving along Highway 141. The cover of the local *Call of the Pewee* monthly paper (December 1977) featured a picture of Trixie:

A full-grown Mediterranean donkey—one of five belonging to Mr. and Mrs. Grove Gleason. There are only a few hundred of these little animals in the United States, as it is impractical to import them from their native islands of Sicily and Sardinia, where they provide the motive power for primary milling devices and haul twigs for small stoves for heating. They take charcoal, fruit and vegetables to market—and then provide transportation to the owner for his return home.

In Sicily, laundry is done at the home of a laundress who places a flat platform on the donkey's back. The folded laundry is placed on the platform, and the laundress rides on top of all, administering an extra press to the clothes she carries back to the owner.

Despite the Miniature's small size, he can pull a considerable load or a cart full of children. These donkeys, which the Gleasons had had for about three months, enjoy a relatively easy life…sharing an ample pasture with two Mexican burros, Sarah and Teresa. The miniatures had been only pasture animals, and were rather wild-like when the Gleasons got them. But with the attention of the Gleasons' grandchildren, 9-year-old Kristen, 7-year-old Cynthia, and 3-year-old Gavin, the little donkeys are becoming tamer. By nature, they are gentle, affectionate animals and make wonderful pets.

The Gleasons' herd include two full-grown Jennets—Fermata and Mamita (one or both is hopefully in foal for the spring); a young Jack, Rickey; and 2 young Jennets named Trixie and Gypsy. When Rickey is 2 years old, he will become head of the herd.

Their adult height, which is 32–37 inches, is not their only distinguishing feature. All have one very prominent marking—a dark strip that runs down the back and across the shoulders to form a cross. The cross is said to be a mark of honor, for Jesus entered Jerusalem on a donkey, and Mary rode a donkey to Bethlehem where Jesus was born.[81]

Also known as **Castlewood**, the **Bondurant-Hustin House** (104 Castlewood Drive) was built by Louisville realtor J.D. Bondurant and his wife, Myrah Gray, in 1885. It is one of very few examples of the Queen Anne style in Pewee Valley and is certainly the best. The two-story frame house is sited on four acres, a tract that retains much of its original landscaping. There is also a historic carriage house on the property; built about 1870, it predates the main house.

The house is built on an asymmetrical plan and has weatherboard siding and a hipped roof with projecting gable wings. A round tower with a conical roof is typical of the Queen Anne style.[82]

Joseph David "J.D." Bondurant (1830–1899) was a native Kentuckian who spent some part of his childhood in Oldham County. He worked as a laborer on his father's farm and then became a farmer himself. In 1863, he was required to register for the Union army draft in Louisville. He duly registered but did not serve. Instead, he covertly supported the Confederacy as a member of a secret society known as the Order of American Knights, which emulated another "Copperhead" group (Copperheads were active Northern supporters of the Confederacy) called the Knights of the Golden Circle. Active in Indiana and Ohio, the Golden Circle aided and abetted John Hunt Morgan, the highly effective raider of the Old Northwest and Kentucky.

The Knights of the Golden Circle and groups with similar names were implicated in what was called the Great Northwestern Conspiracy of 1864, which was a Confederate plot to raid, plunder, and burn Chicago while also storming the large POW camp there and liberating Confederate prisoners. In a report to Union provost marshal Colonel J.P. Sanders in Missouri, J.D. Bondurant was among those named as a conspirator by virtue of his membership in the Order of American Knights.[83] There is no record of his having been apprehended, detained, or otherwise punished. Most likely, he was not, since Federal prosecutors had their hands full and focused on the organization's officers and ringleaders. In any case, after the Civil War, Bondurant resumed his prosperous business selling seeds and general agricultural supplies in Louisville. He was still in this business according to the 1870 census but, by 1881, left the wholesale trade and went into real estate and was prospering well into the 1890s:

There are in the city a number of substantial and representative firms devoting their attention to transactions in real estate and real estate investments. One of the best known and most successful of these is that of J.D. Bondurant & Co., conducting business with offices at 355 Fifth street; the members of the firm being Messrs. J.D. Bondurant, J.S. Miller and W.T. James. Mr. Bondurant established this business about ten years ago, under its present style, and the other members becoming associated with him during the third year. The firm does an active business in all departments of general real estate agency, buying and selling real estate on commission, negotiating loans on real estate securities, selling real estate notes or cashing them, making investments for non-residents or other capitalists, taking entire charge of properties for sale and looking after every detail, and in every way giving efficient attention to every interest confided to their charge. They have at all times on hand and for sale a desirable list of property in the city and its vicinity, suitable either for manufacturing, business or residence purposes, including in their offerings many of the most attractive bargains now in the market; and they are prepared to undertake the disposition of real estate, either at private sale or by auction, giving prompt attention to every commission and in every way rendering efficient service to their patrons. Mr. Bondurant of this firm is a native of Kentucky and was engaged in the agricultural and hardware business in this city, previous to starting in the real estate business in 1870, and Mr. W.T. James is the son of Thomas J. James, in the coal business, and is a young and enterprising business man, and in every way the firm combines every element of experience and efficiency necessary to the success of the enterprise, and enjoys a most excellent reputation for the reliability and accuracy of its dealing.[84]

The **Joseph H. Ellis House** (320 Maple Avenue), according to its nomination to the National Register of Historic Places, was either built "or substantially remodeled about 1890....Located in the area of town laid out in 1866 by Henry Smith, the property provides one of the few remaining

The Joseph H. Ellis House was built (or extensively remodeled) around 1890. Its Queen Anne styling was influenced by the Villa Ridge Inn, which was built in 1889. *Pewee Valley Historical Society.*

intact examples of pre-1900 houses…[and] is representative of the large rambling residences…influenced by the town's new Queen Anne style hotel, the Villa Ridge Inn, built in 1889."[85]

Joseph H. Ellis was fourth vice president of the Louisville and Nashville Railroad (under President Milton H. Smith). He was one of numerous L&N senior employees who had either full-time homes or summer homes in Pewee Valley by the end of the nineteenth century and beginning of the twentieth. The *Courier-Journal* identified the Ellises as prominent among the town's permanent residents. Ellis, who was well known for his fine library, was president of the town's Shakespeare Club.[86] Late in 1902, he and his family moved to Knoxville, Tennessee, after he received a promotion:

> *Knoxville, Tenn., Nov. 1—(Special)—*
>
> *J.H. Ellis to-day assumed his duties as vice president and general manager of the Atlanta, Knoxville and Northern branch of the Louisville and Nashville railroad. He at once issued a circular announcing these appointments: R. Montford, chief engineer, office at Louisville; W.H. Courtenay, principal assistant engineer, office at Louisville; C.W Bradley, superintendent, office at Blue Ridge, Ga.; N.H. Brown, master of trains, office at Blue Ridge, Ga. Mr. Bradshaw arrived yesterday from Russellville, Ky., and began his duties today.[87]*

The Ellis House was sold to industrialist J.W. Stine Jr., and his wife, Julia Omberg Stine, in 1902 for $4,630. They owned it for the next thirteen years.

The **Forrester-Duvall House** (115 Old Forest Road), a two-story frame home, is conspicuous among Pewee Valley houses as among its few large Craftsman-style structures. It was built about 1908 by Walter Shelby Forrester (1861–1944) and his wife, Julia Lockhart Nelson Forrester (circa 1864–1934), on what was originally fourteen acres. It is believed that the Forresters built it on spec, as they were living elsewhere in Pewee Valley at the time.

A printer by trade, Forrester also served as assistant adjutant general on the staff of Governor William O'Connell Bradley. He was appointed in 1895. Three years later, at the start of the Spanish-American War, the governor assigned him to command Camp Wilbur Smith, which was set up about three miles from his Pewee Valley home in the fall of 1898, when Bradley called up the State Guard for possible national service.

Forrester sent a telegram to the camp's namesake, General Wilbur Smith, the state's adjutant general, inviting him to visit the encampment:

Pewee Valley, Ky., September 25, 1898.

Forrester Guards and Bradley Guards, now in Camp Wilbur Smith, extend invitation to Governor and yourself to visit us.

General Smith accepted, and Forrester and his aides met him at the Pewee Valley depot. They accompanied him

to the grove where the Pewee Valley and Lexington Companies received them at a given point and were escorted to the splendid grounds by Colonel Forrester to witness drills, maneuvers, target practice and sham battles.

Nearly one thousand spectators, including one hundred college girls, sang their college songs, and bedecked the officers with college colors of blue and buff. Considering that these soldiers were new recruits after nearly four thousand had gone to the front, their drills and maneuvers were considered excellent. On September 28, 1898, Capt. Cassidy's Company was awarded the gold medal given by General Smith for best drilled men. The cost of this encampment for about ten days was about one thousand dollars.[88]

One of Pewee Valley's few large Craftsman-style houses, the Forrester-Duvall House was built about 1908. *Pewee Valley Historical Society.*

The Locust (6917 LaGrange Road) is one of Pewee Valley's oldest surviving homes. Portions of it go as far back as 1819 or even earlier. The nomination submitted to the National Register of Historic Places in 1975 calls it "an interesting example of the evolution of architecture in Kentucky. The house spans several different periods, from the early settlement through the Victorian era to the 20th century." The nomination elaborates: "The property on which the Locust is built was originally part of a 4,000-acre land grant which was granted to Samuel Beall in 1784 by Patrick Henry," who was at the time in his second term as governor of Virginia, which in those days included Kentucky before it entered the Union in 1792.

> Beall sold several hundred acres of the land to George Nicholas (?–1799), the prominent lawyer and first Attorney General of Kentucky. Nicholas never paid the purchase price and contracted 200 acres to Robert Wooden, who took possession of the land during Nicholas' lifetime and made valuable improvements on it. The date of the deed is 1819. It is indicated that this is probably when the stone portion of the house was constructed, although there is a tradition that this structure and the stone springhouse nearby date from considerably earlier. The house changed owners many times after 1834 when Robert Wooden sold it to John Howell. In 1850 the estate, which included a number of slaves, was auctioned. The auction was the result of a suit filed by the owner's wife, Ann Gough, against her husband and his heirs. It took place in compliance with an order of the Oldham County Court. After the auction the house changed hands several times, until 1857 when Jonas H. Rhorer purchased the property.[89]

This long history, entwined with the making of the nation, is all well and good, but many people know The Locust from its role in Annie Fellows Johnston's "Little Colonel" books, where it figures as the setting for many events. Johnston uses it as the home of Old Colonel Lloyd—and for good reason. George Washington Weissinger, the author's inspiration for the Old Colonel, boarded at The Locust during part of the 1890s, though he never owned the house. When Annie Johnston was interviewed in the June 2, 1907 issue of the *San Antonio Light*, she held up a photo of The Locust and commented to the reporter, "Here on the gallery at the end of the long avenue of locusts, the Old Colonel would sit and watch the passors by [sic] through his spy glass."[90]

FAITH AND FREEDOM

Together, tiny Pewee Valley's remarkable pair of historic districts creates a rare real-time portrait of the turn-of-the-century emergence of the American suburb. In its Kentucky incarnation, this pioneering suburb transformed a pleasant woodland into a fairyland just a short rail ride from the bustling summer swelter of Louisville.

But on the periphery of incorporated Pewee Valley, there were two communities that found no place on the National Register. These are Frazier Town and Stumptown, which, shortly after the Civil War, were built by Black men and women in the neighborhoods around a core of Black churches.

Frazier Town came to life in the early 1870s, just outside Pewee Valley's city limits off Rollington Road, near the county line. By 1879, it appears in the *Beers & Lanagan Atlas of Pewee Valley* as a collection of just nine dwellings near Sycamore Methodist Chapel, which the atlas identifies only as a "Colored Church."[91] Before the church was built, Black Baptist and Methodist congregations shared a combined church and school located on Old Floydsburg Road in Stumptown, which was built and financed by the Reconstruction-era federal Freedmen's Bureau in 1869. Katie S. Smith, in her *Pewee Valley: Land of the Little Colonel* (1974), notes, "In the early 1870s, members [in Frazier Town] began to consider the possibility of constructing their own church building. Land was difficult to acquire. However, Mrs.

Sycamore Chapel dates to 1873 in the Black community of Frazier Town, just outside the Pewee Valley city limits. *Pewee Valley Historical Society.*

Brenner of Louisville gave land for the new church. Sycamore Chapel was organized and built in 1873."[92]

Locals have long said that Frazier Town was named in honor of Bartlett Frazier, a freedman landowner in the area who, in 1870, lived in Pewee Valley at Clovercroft, where he "work[ed] in the garden." At the time, the estate belonged to Milton M. Rhorer.

The Rhorers left Clovercroft and Pewee Valley for California in 1874, by which time Bartlett Frazier and his wife, Mary (they had been married since 1863), owned land in what became Frazier Town. Between 1870 and 1874, they had accumulated two and a half acres, on which they lived. Bartlett worked as a farm laborer and Mary as a laundress. The property remained in the Frazier family until Mary died on July 2, 1912, Bartlett having died before 1910. Mary left the property to her Frazier Town neighbors, as a copy of her will, dated May 17, 1912, and preserved in the Oldham County Courthouse, attests:

> *I Mary Frazier being of sound mind and body hereby make my last will and testament leaving all my property consisting of two acres of land and house and all furniture upon to the May [F]lower [T]emple No 99 after the Mortgage and accrued interest has been paid holder of the Mortgage being Mrs. Lavenia Watson Cooper of Louisville. The temple having liberty to dispose of all the remaining property as they see fit after a tomb stone has been placed over the graves of my husband and self and after all other expenses has been paid.*[93]

Lifelong, the Fraziers were leaders in the freedmen's community, both in Frazier Town and Stumptown, which was the home of the Pewee Valley First Baptist Church, located at 7104 Old Floydsburg Road. Built in 1869, it predates Sycamore Chapel and was established by the Freedmen's Bureau as a combined school and church.[94] The school was built on part of the church's land, which the church leased to the school for ninety-nine years. The cost to build the school was $292.50.[95]

The First Baptist Church was 135 years old when fire struck on August 17, 2003. The *Louisville Courier-Journal* reported the story the next day:

> *The blaze began about 1:45 a.m. in the rear of the original church, which was built in 1869....Flames gutted the structure and charred wooden pews. But the newer and larger worship hall, which is about 35 feet from the original building, is unharmed.*

Pewee Valley First Baptist Church was built in 1869 in the Black community of Stumptown by the Reconstruction-era Freedmen's Bureau as a combined school and church. It was 135 years old in 2003 when it was swept by fire that destroyed the original portion of the structure. *Pewee Valley Historical Society.*

Firefighters from the Pewee Valley, Worthington, South Oldham, Anchorage and Middletown departments had the blaze under control by 4 a.m....

The destruction of the original church, a portion of which was built by former slaves, is a severe loss for the county's African-American community, historian Dorothy Lammlein says....

Though he lamented the loss of the building, the Rev. Henry Ford, Jr., the pastor, said, "It's just a building; it's not people."

Alisa Durham, 42, grew up in the church. Her grandmother was married there and her uncles served as deacons. Other relatives were founders of the church.

"This is our life," she said, looking at what remained yesterday morning.

Calling the small congregation very close to one another, Ford said, "Everybody knows everybody, and if you stay around long enough, you'll probably become kin to somebody."

The community around the church is just as close, and that's going to help the church through this situation, he said. While church members were cleaning up yesterday, a woman stopped by and handed Ford a check for $250, saying she drives by the landmark almost every day.[96]

Chapter 8

THE REIGN OF THE LITTLE COLONEL

P ewee Valley has been the home of numerous writers, but the most famous by far was and remains Annie Fellows Johnston. Her "Little Colonel" book series consists of thirteen titles plus a paper-doll book and a few other related volumes, all published out of Boston by the L.C. Page Company between 1896 and 1912.[97] In 1935—twenty-three years after the last book in the series, *Mary Ware's Promised Land*, appeared, and four years after the author's death—"America's Little Darling," Shirley Temple, appeared in *The Little Colonel*, released by Fox Film Corp. Critic Andre Sennwald reviewed it in the *New York Times* on March 25, 1935. He pronounced it "all adrip with magnolia whimsy and vast, unashamed portions of synthetic Dixie atmosphere," condemning it for being "so ruthless in its exploitation of Miss Temple's great talent for infant charm that it seldom succeeds in being properly lively and gay." And yet he ended the review by noting that the audience applauded for eleven seconds (apparently film critics timed these things back in 1935) after the final fade-out and judged that the film "ought to bring out the best in everyone who sees it."[98] The film is shown on television to this day and is available for streaming. While millions have seen the movie, millions more know it only by the iconic staircase tap dance between Shirley and Bill "Bojangles" Robinson—which is not only charming but was also the first interracial dance pairing in the history of Hollywood. (Fox cut it out in reels sent to the southern states.)

The movie was based on the first book, *The Little Colonel* (1895), of what would become a thirteen-book series with many characters, plotlines, and themes. But the story told in this debut volume has all the elements that give the series its staying power. The place is Lloydsborough Valley, a fictional Kentucky town based entirely on Pewee Valley. The time is the 1870s, the decade following the Civil War, which deeply divided the United States, Kentucky, and many families. One such family is headed by Colonel Lloyd, the "Old Colonel," a dyed-in-the-gray-wool Confederate. After his daughter, Elizabeth Lloyd, elopes with a Yankee, Jack Sherman, the Old Colonel effectively disowns her. Six years of estrangement pass. Jack goes off prospecting, and Elizabeth returns to Lloydsborough Valley with her charmingly rambunctious daughter, formally named Lloyd and familiarly known as the Little Colonel. The girl's initial meeting with the Old Colonel does not go well, but the two soon grow close—their stubborn natures uniting them. Jack Sherman returns from his prospecting venture, and the future of the extended family is cast into doubt. In the fullness of time, the Little Colonel's unconquerable spirit overmatches the Old Colonel's bitter obstinacy, and the novel ends in reconciliation.

The Little Colonel is a well-told story with highly sympathetic characters. It is also a story with themes that all enduring stories share—love, disruption, despair, disappointment, anger, and reconciliation. Is it "great literature"? Well, the glib answer is that Annie Fellows Johnston is no Leo Tolstoy. But the truth is that Pewee Valley's Johnston does invite comparison with Russia's Tolstoy, and her "Little Colonel" series, in some ways, holds its own against *War and Peace.*

Don't laugh. In 1,392 pages (Oxford World Classics translation), Tolstoy boldly merged fact and fiction in an epic that unfolds across the Russian empire (population 35,005,000 over 22,400,000 square miles)[99] during the Napoleonic Wars. In 1,833 pages (*The Complete Little Colonel Series by Annie Fellows Johnston*, 2012 Kindle edition), Johnston boldly merged fact and fiction in a series of books set in a version of Pewee Valley (2022 estimated population 1,618 over 1.93 square miles), which she called Lloydsborough Valley, in the years following the Civil War. Today, the wooden signs that mark Pewee Valley's boundaries on LaGrange Road/Highway 146 proclaim it the "Land of the Little Colonel."[100]

Bigger Than *War and Peace*

War and Peace was published in 1869, and scholars have been tracing, connecting, and untangling Tolstoy's tightly woven strands of fact and fiction ever since. The passionate avocation of my late wife, Donna Russell, was the Pewee Valley Historical Society and her own pursuit of Pewee Valley's history. In 2014, she gave a PowerPoint presentation to the Louisville Genealogical Society titled "Annie Fellows Johnston's Little Colonel Series: What Was Real?" Her purpose was to both connect and untangle the strands of fact and fiction in Johnston's series of books, which, taken together, dwarf Tolstoy's masterpiece in sheer page count.

Annie Fellows Johnston herself was a bit annoyed by the repeated question, "What was real?" In chapter 8 of *The Land of the Little Colonel*, an autobiography published in 1929 while she was living at The Beeches in Pewee Valley, Johnston wrote:

> *It is a gratification to know that the various characters have become so endeared to their readers that they count them as warm personal friends. To be sure, it often becomes annoying when a* [fan] *letter contains six or seven pages of closely written questions.... The writers do not seem to realize that many of the characters and incidents are purely imaginary, but insist on having their curiosity satisfied, just as if the happenings were in real life.*

The basic facts of Johnston's connection to Pewee Valley merit a quick recap. She was born (1863) and raised in McCutchanville, Indiana. As an adult, she lived in nearby Evansville, where she married Reverend William Levi Johnston, a widower with three children, Mary, Rena, and John. The reverend's first wife, Hallie Eaves Johnston, had suffered from tuberculosis, and the three children were sent to Pewee Valley to live with their aunt Rena (Eaves) and uncle Albert W. Burge. After Hallie died in 1883 and Annie married Reverend Johnston, the children continued to spend summers with their aunt and uncle in Pewee. Then, in 1892, William Johnston succumbed to tuberculosis himself, and Annie now found herself responsible for her three stepchildren. She turned to writing to support her family. In 1895, she visited Pewee Valley for the first time, where she stayed with the Burges. In her 1929 autobiography, she recalled her first encounter with people of this place, this cast of "characters" who would feed her creativity through a baker's dozen of highly successful books:

Along this street one summer morning, nearly thirty years ago, came stepping an old Confederate Colonel. Every one greeted him deferentially. He was always pointed out to new comers. Some people called attention to him because he had given his right arm to the lost cause, some because they thought he resembled Napoleon, and others because they had some amusing tale to tell of his eccentricities. He was always clad in white duck in the summer, and was wrapped in a picturesque military cape in the winter.

This morning a child of delicate flower-like beauty walked beside him. She was pushing a doll buggy in which rode a parrot that had lost some of its tail feathers, and at her heels trailed a Scotch and Skye terrier.

"She's her grandfather all over again," remarked a lady in one of the carriages, "temper, lordly manners, imperious ways and all. I call her 'The Little Colonel.' There's a good title for you, Cousin Anne. Put her in a book."

And so she did—along with many others she encountered in Pewee Valley. Most of her models, however, were members of three families: the Weissingers, Muirs, and Craigs.

Among the Weissingers, George Washington Weissinger Jr. was Johnston's inspiration for the Old Colonel, and the portrait of his wife, Grandmother Amanthus, was the real-life George's real-life wife, Amelia Neville Pearce Weissinger. The Weissingers' daughter, Ann Amelia, married John Hoadley Cochran. Their daughter, Harriet—called Hattie—was born on November 24, 1890. Hattie, whose married name was Hattie Cochran Dick, was the inspiration for Little Colonel Lloyd Sherman, and her parents, the Shermans, were inspired by Ann and John.

George Washington Jr.'s sister Blanche, who was born about 1840, married Captain Thomas Floyd Smith on January 21, 1858. After the Civil War, the family moved from Missouri to Pewee Valley, where they lived at Beechmore. Blanche, who was Hattie's real-life great-aunt, inspired the character of Great-Aunt Sally Tyler in *The Little Colonel*. A portrait of her husband, which hung at Beechmore, inspired the portrait of "Tom," the Old Colonel's son, who was killed fighting for the Confederacy.

The Muirs supplied more characters for the "Little Colonel" books. Judge Peter B. Muir was the source of the fictional Judge Moore, whose deceased wife was called "Phronie" in the books. Short for Sephronia, this was the real name of the real wife of Peter B. Muir. Anna Burge Muir Humphrey was the first cousin of Hallie Louise Burge Jacob and the inspiration for the

Annie Fellows Johnston (holding the parasol) is seen here with Hattie Cochran, her inspiration for the character of the "Little Colonel" herself, Lloyd Sherman (played by Shirley Temple in the 1935 movie). *Pewee Valley Historical Society.*

fictional Anna Moore, first cousin of Rob Moore and Judge Moore. Muir Semple, the son of Lillian Muir and Alexander Latimer Semple, was the first cousin of Anna Burge Muir Humphrey. He inspired the creation of Rob Moore, Judge Moore's grandson. Rob ended up marrying Lloyd Sherman, the Little Colonel herself.

From the Craigs, Annie McCown Craig (wife of Aleck Craig) emerges as the inspiration for Grandmother McIntrye, the mistress of Edgewood. Fannie Craig, daughter of Annie and Aleck, was the model for the stories' schoolteacher, Miss Allison. Mary Craig, oldest child of Annie and Aleck, and Major General Henry Ware Lawton inspired the creation of Johnston's Walton family. The Lawtons' eldest son, Manley, found expression in fiction

Fannie Craig, shown here in a photograph by Kate Matthews, was the inspiration for Miss Allison, the schoolteacher in *The Little Colonel. Pewee Valley Historical Society.*

as Ranald Walton, aka "The Little Captain," which was his nickname in real life. The Lawton girls—Frances Lawton Grayhart, Katherine Lawton, and Elise Lawton Bagby—spawned fictional doppelgangers in Allison, Kitty, and Elise Walton.

Louise Craig and Samuel Culbertson inspired Uncle Sidney and Aunt Elise, while William and Alexander Culbertson, sons of Louise and Samuel, were the models for the "Two Little Knights of Kentucky," Keith and Malcolm McIntrye.

PEWEE VALLEY GOES HOLLYWOOD

The son of Blanche Washington Smith and Captain Thomas Floyd Smith, Karl J. Smith, a mapmaker, illustrator, commercial, and heraldic artist,[101] designed the Little Colonel game. Yes! Pewee Valley not only was depicted in a popular series of books and in a movie based on the first book of that series but was also the inspiration for a board game, which Smith designed after *The Little Colonel* film had become a national sensation.

Annie Fellows Johnston died, at home in Pewee Valley, on October 5, 1931, four years before Fox Film's *The Little Colonel* had its premiere in Louisville at the Rialto Theatre on February 22, 1935. The negotiations with Fox Film Corp. for the movie rights to Johnston's 1895 novel were handled by Annie's stepdaughter Mary G. Johnston. Part of the contract with the studio was delivery of a "scrapbook" of photos showing the local Pewee Valley people and places that inspired Annie Fellows Johnston to write the book on which the film was based. Fox wanted the pictures to guide its set and costume designers. The scrapbook was assembled by Mrs. Thomas Moore, who had the title of managing director of Little Colonel Incorporated, which owned the rights to all the Little Colonel intellectual property. The cover letter she wrote in transmitting the scrapbook to Fox explained that the photographs were "not obtained by a cameraman but by climbing attic stairs and having reproductions made of dusty treasured bundles." Many of the images turned over to the studio production department were copies of the work of Pewee Valley's photographer-in-residence Kate Matthews. With considerable understanding, Mrs. Moore explained:

> *Since the author created neither the environment nor the character, but made them living and vital for the rest of us through her accurate portrayal of real people and real places, it occurred to me that actual photographs of such characters and places might be a medium through which a clever director would find the essence of what has made "The Little Colonel" such a potent factor in the lives of two generations of Americans. The Photographs were not obtained by a cameraman but by climbing attic stairs and having reproductions made of dusty treasured bundles.*
>
> *Every year since the book was first published, thousands of children have come to Pewee Valley to see where the Little Colonel really lived. For their sake, I cannot but fervently hope that the motion picture will faithfully follow the book. Children are peculiarly literal and loyal and demand what they love and remember.*[102]

Rebecca Porter, photographed by Kate Matthews, was the model for "Mom Beck" in Annie Fellows Johnston's *The Little Colonel. Pewee Valley Historical Society.*

A rumor quickly spread that *The Little Colonel* had been shot on-location in Pewee Valley. As is true of many rumors, this assertion assumed over the years the mythic status of unquestioned truth. In fact, the movie was not shot on-location at all, and Shirley Temple never even set foot in Pewee Valley. In 2008, the Pewee Valley Historical Society invited her to its Little Colonel event, but Shirley Temple Black's health prevented her coming. She passed on four years later, on February 11, 2012, at the age of eighty-five.[103]

Amid the movie's popularity, leading game maker Selchow & Righter, a firm that would go on to create Parcheesi, Scrabble, and Trivial Pursuit, turned Karl Smith's board design into a colorful board game.

The board was a pictorial map of Lloydsborough Valley (the fictional alter ego of Pewee Valley) on which cut-out game pieces based on the movie's characters moved. There were Fritz, the Little Colonel's Skye terrier, and the Little Colonel herself. There were also the Little Colonel's father, Lloyd Sherman; her grandfather "Old Colonel" Lloyd; her mother, Mrs. Sherman; Walker, the Old Colonel's manservant; Mom Beck, the Little Colonel's nurse; and May Lilly and Henry Clay, the Little Colonel's playmates. These figures were moved around the "points of interest" depicted on the board. These mostly bore the real names of actual Pewee Valley locations, including Locust, Tanglewood, Oaklea, the Episcopal church, Undulata, The Beeches, The Gables, Edgewood, Beechmore, "Stumptown" Baptist Church, the home of Gay Melville, the post office, the inn, the Presbyterian Church, Lloydsborough Seminary (the Kentucky College for Young Ladies), Clovercroft, the railroad station, and the "Home of the Little Colonel." Delacoosha was depicted as well, the home in which Annie Fellows Johnston first encountered many of the people who inspired the characters of the Little Colonel (1895).

FUN AND GAMES

The Selchow & Righter game was not the only spinoff the Little Colonel stories spawned. McLoughlin Bros., Inc., a New York publisher specializing in the color printing of children's books, puzzles, games, paper soldiers, and paper dolls, was the first "media" company to purchase rights to Little Colonel products. In 1908, McLoughlin Bros. took out an ad in *Publishers Weekly*, volume 73, page 971, introducing a Little Colonel card game for older children and blocks and scroll puzzles for younger kids. The ad copy is revealing:

> BASED ON THE LITTLE COLONEL STORIES.
> *The remarkable extent to which the vividly drawn characters of Mrs. Johnston's popular Little Colonel Stories have become like familiar acquaintances to a vast section of the juvenile reading public, has suggested the idea that a card game in which the leading personages and places of the stories were introduced would furnish a pleasant and acceptable pastime to a large proportion of her multitude of readers. A game has accordingly been devised, and is now offered to the public, which, it is believed, will be found to possess playing qualities sufficiently good to*

Promotional flyer for *The Little Colonel*, released by Fox Films in 1935. *Pewee Valley Historical Society.*

make it interesting even to players not acquainted with the Little Colonel
Stories, while those who are familiar with them will, of course, have their
enjoyment greatly heightened by being reminded of delightful hours spent
over Mrs. Johnston's charming pages.
Price 50 Cents

Little Colonel
BLOCKS AND SCROLL PUZZLES FOR THE YOUNGER CHILDREN.
For little folk too young to care for the card game, some very handsome
Blocks and Scroll Puzzles have been gotten up. The pictures illustrate the
earliest book, which treats of the Little Colonel's baby days. The set of
Blocks consists of 20 cubes, each 2-inches square, done in lithography.
The Scroll Puzzles are put up in three different sets, each consisting of two
dissected puzzle pictures,
Price, Set of Blocks, $1.50; Scroll Puzzles, 75 cents each

McLoughlin Bros. was serious about selling its goods. A wholesale order
list shows that the scroll puzzles wholesaled for ninety-six dollars a gross, and
the card game sold for seventy-two dollars a gross.[104]

Over the years, doll manufacturers produced many Shirley Temple dolls,
including those dressed in Little Colonel fashions. These include dolls from
an unknown manufacturer in the 1930s; from the Danbury Mint, circa
1995; and from the Ideal Toy Company in 1982.[105]

LAND OF THE LITTLE COLONEL

Some modern scholars criticize "Johnston's land of the Little Colonel
[for perpetuating] the ideals of southern patriarchy of the 1850s" and
glorifying antebellum Kentucky "as a place full of colored people and
pretty girls and polite men."[106] But contemporaries found in the stories
deeper value. "Describing the author as possessing 'a rare gift in producing
little stories in the nature of allegories full of spiritual significance and
beauty,' the *Boston Transcript* hailed [Johnston] as 'the most gifted and the
most helpful of the present-day writers for young people.'"[107] And novelist
Alice Hegan Rice (1870–1942), in her introduction to Johnston's *The Land
of the Little Colonel*, wrote:

Hundreds of thousands of girls have met their own problems in the problems of their favorite heroines. They have seen the first perplexities of life faced beautifully and spiritually; they have seen that stupid little word "duty" glorified into something fine and noble; they have seen the small and seemingly insignificant things of life take on a new and beautiful dignity.[108]

Johnston received thousands of letters expressing such sentiments as this, from a Chicago girl: "I know a great many girls who take the 'Little Colonel' for their model and seek to copy her." Or this, from a New Yorker: "You will never know how much higher I have tried to build since your books have come to us." From a twelve-year-old Tennessean:

I learned to love and appreciate my own mother more[,] to love my little chums more, to see the beauty even, in the tall oaks and locusts, and listen to their voices, as I read deeper and deeper into the heart of those books.... In fact, where is the little girl that doesn't aspire to higher ideals, when they read your books?[109]

Sue Lynn McDaniel, a scholar at Western Kentucky University, characterized the Little Colonel as a full-blown popular culture phenomenon: "Although modern readers question many of the values taught by Annie Fellows Johnston in the Little Colonel series," she wrote, "the impact of the literature on numerous turn-of-the-century children and succeeding generations cannot be doubted."[110] Through the Little Colonel, Pewee Valley itself has become a presence in American popular culture.

PEWEE FOREVER

Pewee Valley is a small place with a big appetite for its rich history. But it is no mere outdoor museum. It is a thriving community, with a population that has grown from just under 1,450 in 2011 to an estimated 1,618 in 2022. If pressed, Peweeans do call their community a suburb. History certainly favors that definition, since the place was one of the first-generation American suburbs, made possible by the short-line railroad service that was available to the community shortly before the midpoint of the nineteenth century. And today, the place has many of the customary suburban businesses, including landscaping and tree-trimming services, a dance/yoga studio, a laser hair-removal emporium, a physical therapy center, an auto repair shop, a veterinary center, a podiatrist, an HVAC contractor, a website designer, realtors, a piano tuner and repair business, housepainters, insurance agencies, a security systems installer, a women's club, and the Little Colonel Players theater group. Of course, supermarkets, pharmacies, and fast food are available a short distance beyond the outskirts of town. And center-city Louisville is just an eighteen-mile drive.

Yet nobody living in Pewee really feels they are suburbanites. Yes, most of the larger estates have been subdivided—but the subdivisions are subject to zoning ordinances intended to preserve the essential rural quality of living here, and as we've seen in chapter 7, many of the houses and other structures of historical and aesthetic value are protected by listing in the National Register of Historic Places. It is a living place, where the past remains a lively presence.

Like the rest of Kentucky, a deeply divided border state, Pewee Valley was caught up in the Civil War, but no great battles were fought here. In fact, no single outstanding historical event unfolded on these 1.93 square miles. Nevertheless, it was a place that inspired and even thrilled its residents. Noble Butler, who gave Pewee Valley its name, also gave it a myth—tongue-in-cheek, to be sure, yet also in earnest. It was an expression of the enchantment those who came here both felt and created. They built beautiful cottages. They painted pictures. They photographed its people and places. They wrote poems. They wrote books, and there was even a Hollywood movie. Then, later, they established a historical society to preserve the record of it, lest, like Camelot or Avalon or maybe Brigadoon, it would someday vanish if no effort were made to record and remember it. The places that we count as special—whether great cities or great natural sites—are always a combination of reality, invention, and imagination. They are as much feeling as fact. And that is Pewee Valley.

By the numbers, Pewee Valley is a peaceful place, a standout in this regard, given the realities of contemporary American life. Demographers calculate annual crime statistics on a standardized "per 100,000 residents." Assault, which in legal language means nothing more or less than causing someone to reasonably fear imminent harm, was most recently reported for Pewee Valley as 125.9 per 100,000 residents versus a national average of 282.7. For the three other categories of major violent crime—murder, rape, and robbery—0 incidents were reported versus national annual figures per 100,000 of 6.1 murders, 40.7 rapes, and 135.5 robberies. Property crimes are also very few in number. The most recent annual incidence of burglary was 63 per 100,000 residents. Theft and motor vehicle theft were reported at 0. The most recent national numbers for burglary are 500.1; for theft, 2,042.8; and for motor vehicle theft, 284—all per 100,000 residents.[111]

Pewee Valley's stats are not miraculous, but I'd wager that those living elsewhere would be very happy if they applied to them. Noble Butler, who had come to Pewee Valley after witnessing the senseless murder of his beloved brother, wrote that the town's namesake, the eastern wood-pewee, had a sweet call, "Pe-wee, Pe-wee," in which he, for one, distinctly heard this message: "Peace and good will, peace and good will."[112] He thought of it as the songlike motto of Pewee Valley. As one who lives here, I agree. It is the sweet essence of the place. Always was, and I hope it will always be.

NOTES

Chapter 1

1. United States Census Bureau, Gazeteer Files, www.census.gov/
geographies/reference-files/time-series/geo/gazetteer-files.html;
World Population Review, "Pewee Valley, Kentucky Population 2023,"
worldpopulationreview.com/us-cities/pewee-valley-ky-population.
2. Data USA, Pewee Valley, KY, datausa.io/profile/geo/pewee-valley-ky;
United States Census Bureau, "Quick Facts: Housing," www.census.gov/
quickfacts/fact/table/US/VET605221.
3. Helen McKinney, "Pewee Valley," Kentucky History, explorekyhistory.
ky.gov/items/show/697.
4. The Cornell Lab, *All About Birds*, "Eastern Wood-Pewee Identification,"
www.allaboutbirds.org/guide/Eastern_Wood-Pewee/id#.
5. [Noble Butler,] *Antiquitates Peweeji* (July 4, 1858), www.peweevalleyhistory.
org/antiquitates.html.
6. Ben Casseday, *Casseday's History of Louisville* (Louisville: Hull & Brother,
1852).
7. Edwin Bryant, *What I Saw in California: Journal of a Tour* (New York: D.
Appleton & Company, 1849).
8. [Catherine Anne Warfield,] *The Household of Bouverie; or, The Elixer of Gold*
(New York: Derby & Jackson, 1860).
9. Pewee Valley Historical Society, "Welcome to the History of Pewee
Valley, Kentucky," www.peweevalleyhistory.org.

10. "An 'E'asy Job," *The Call of the Pewee* 1, no. 3 (August 1969), 4, www.peweevalleyhistory.org/call-1969.html.
11. Pewee Valley Historical Society, "Welcome to the History of Pewee Valley."

Chapter 2

12. Alan Axelrod, "John Filson," in *American Writers of the Early Republic, Dictionary of Literary Biography*, vol. 37, ed. Emory Elliott (Detroit: Gale Research, 1985), 158–60.
13. John Filson, *The Discovery, Settlement and Present State of Kentucke* (Wilmington, DE: Printed by James Adams, 1784), 5–6, 21–22, 29.
14. Charles B. Castner, "Louisville & Frankfort Railroad," in *Encyclopedia of Louisville* (Lexington: University Press of Kentucky), 549.
15. *A Place Called Pewee Valley* (n.p., 1970), [5], www.peweevalleyhistory.org/place-called-pewee-valley.html; Kate Snyder Smith, "Henry Smith (December 4, 1802–March 3, 1883): City Father," Pewee Valley Historical Society, www.peweevalleyhistory.org/henry-smith.html.
16. Pewee Valley Historical Society, "Rollington," www.peweevalleyhistory.org/rollington.html.
17. Ibid.
18. Information on Henry Smith is drawn from Pewee Valley Historical Society, "Henry Smith (December 4, 1802–March 3, 1883): City Father," www.peweevalleyhistory.org/henry-smith.html.
19. Ibid.
20. Pewee Valley Historical Society, "Woodside Cottage: Thomas & Nannette Smith Years," www.peweevalleyhistory.org/woodside.html.
21. Ibid.
22. Bemersyde is named after the famed sixteenth-century estate in Melrose, Roxburghshire, Scotland; see "Bemersyde House & Grounds," www.historichouses.org/house/bemersyde-house/history.
23. Pewee Valley Historical Society, "Bemersyde," www.peweevalleyhistory.org/bemersyde.html.
24. Pewee Valley Historical Society, "Walter Newman Haldeman (April 27, 1821–May 13, 1902): Founder & Publisher of *The Courier-Journal* and *Louisville Times*," www.peweevalleyhistory.org/walter-haldeman.html.
25. Pewee Valley Historical Society, "Tuliphurst: The Dulaney Years & Beyond," www.peweevalleyhistory.org/tuliphurst-the-dulaney-years.

html; postcard [1934] featuring the Welsworth Hotel, i.pinimg.com/orig
inals/20/34/09/20340949b60a90711305ba1eba10dc29.jpg.

26. Pewee Valley Historical Society, "Tuliphurst Manor Subdivision 1955,"
www.peweevalleyhistory.org/sub-tuliphurst.html.

27. Pewee Valley Historical Society, "Clovercroft," www.peweevalleyhistory.
org/clovercroft.html; Pewee Valley Historical Society, "Kate
Matthews—Camera Artist (August 13, 1870–July 5, 1956)," www.
peweevalleyhistory.org/kate-matthews.html.

28. Pewee Valley Historical Society, "Kentucky College for Young Ladies,"
www.peweevalleyhistory.org/ky-college-for-young-ladies.html.

29. Pewee Valley Historical Society, "Peewee Valley First Baptist Church &
Colored School," www.peweevalleyhistory.org/pewee-valley-first-baptist-
church.html.

30. Pewee Valley Historical Society, "Peewee Valley Train Depot," www.
peweevalleyhistory.org/train-depot.html.

31. Pewee Valley Historical Society, "1870. AN ACT to Incorporate the
Town of Pewee Valley, in Oldham County," www.peweevalleyhistory.
org/act-to-incorporate-pewee-valley.html.

32. Pewee Valley Historical Society, "Pewee Valley Cemetery," www.
peweevalleyhistory.org/pewee-valley-cemetery.html.

Chapter 3

33. Charles B. Castner, "Louisville & Frankfort Railroad," in *Encyclopedia of
Louisville* (Lexington: University Press of Kentucky), 549.

34. Max Roser, Esteban Ortiz-Ospina, and Hannah Ritchie, *Life Expectancy*,
ourworldindata.org/life-expectancy#how-did-life-expectancy-change-
over-time.

35. "Crawford, Thomas Howell," in *Encyclopedia of Louisville* (Lexington:
University Press of Kentucky, 2001), 230.

36. Pewee Valley Historical Society, "Kentucky College for Young Ladies,"
www.peweevalleyhistory.org/ky-college-for-young-ladies.html.

37. Ibid.

38. Edgar A. Poe, "A Chapter on Autography [part II]," *Graham's Magazine*
(December 1841), 19:273–86, www.eapoe.org/works/misc/autogc2.
htm#gallagwd.

39. Pewee Valley Historical Society, "Kentucky College for Young Ladies."

Chapter 4

40. Lansford W. Hastings, *The Emigrants' Guide to Oregon and California* (Cincinnati, OH: George Conclin, 1845), 137–38.
41. Edwin Bryant, *What I Saw in California* (1848; New York: D. Appleton, 1849), www.gutenberg.org/ebooks/13002.
42. Katie Snyder Smith, *Pewee Valley: Land of the Little Colonel* (n.p., 1974).
43. Noble Butler, *Antiquitates Peweeji* (July 4, 1858), 11, www.peweevalleyhistory.org/antiquitates.html.
44. Pewee Valley Historical Society, "Edwin Bryant (August 21, 1805–December 16, 1869)," www.peweevalleyhistory.org/edwin-bryant.html.
45. "Judge Peter Brown Muir," ancestors.familysearch.org/en/LCQ4-Y34/judge-peter-brown-muir-1822-1911.
46. Kentucky Online Arts Resource Blog, "Brrr, It's Cold Outside…," kentuckyonlinearts.wordpress.com/2013/02/05/brrr-its-cold-outside.
47. Pewee Valley Historical Society, "Beechmore: The Southers and the Warfields," www.peweevalleyhistory.org/beechmore-souther.html; "Warfield, Catherine (Ann) Ware," Encyclopedia.com, www.encyclopedia.com/arts/news-wires-white-papers-and-books/warfield-catherine-ann-ware.
48. Pewee Valley Historical Society, "Beechmore."
49. "Walker Percy," Wikipedia, en.wikipedia.org/wiki/Walker_Percy; "William Alexander Percy," Wikipedia, en.wikipedia.org/wiki/William_Alexander_Percy.
50. "Walker Percy," Wikipedia, en.wikipedia.org/wiki/Walker_Percy; "William Alexander Percy," Wikipedia, en.wikipedia.org/wiki/William_Alexander_Percy.

Chapter 5

51. Charles B. Dew, "Lincoln and the Border States: Preserving the Union," *Civil War Book Review* (Winter 2012): 1, digitalcommons.lsu.edu/cgi/viewcontent.cgi?article=2663&context=cwbr.
52. Pewee Valley Historical Society, "Walter Newman Haldeman."
53. Pewee Valley Historical Society, "Rosswoods: The Van Horne–Ross House," www.peweevalleyhistory.org/rosswoods.html.
54. Ibid.

55. Unless otherwise noted, material relating to the Kentucky Confederate Home is from Pewee Valley Historical Society, "Kentucky Confederate Home," www.peweevalleyhistory.org/kentucky-confederate-home.html.

56. Rusty Williams, articles in *The Call of the Pewee* (December 2009, January 2010, and February 2010), republished in Pewee Valley Historical Society, "Kentucky Confederate Home."

57. Pewee Valley Historical Society, "What Became of the Confederate Home," www.peweevalleyhistory.org/what-became-of-the-home.html.

58. Ibid.

59. Ibid.

60. *Courier-Journal*, April 28, 1937.

61. Pewee Valley Historical Society, "What Became of the Confederate Home."

Chapter 6

62. Shannon Lee, "How Old Are America's Houses?" Old House Web, www.oldhouseweb.com/how-to-advice/how-old-are-americas-houses.shtml; Southdown Homes, "What Is the Average Lifespan of a House?" southdownhomes.com/what-is-the-average-lifespan-of-a-house.

63. The main source for this section is National Register of Historic Places Registration Form (June 23, 1989), "Central Avenue Historic District," available at Pewee Valley Historical Society, "Pewee Valley National Register Properties and Historic Districts," www.peweevalleyhistory.org/national-register.html.

64. Pewee Valley Historical Society, "Woodside Cottage: Thomas & Nannette Smith Years," www.peweevalleyhistory.org/woodside.html.

65. *Daily Democrat*, November 27, 1858, www.peweevalleyhistory.org/woodside.html.

66. See also Andrew Henderson, "Pewee Valley Celebrates 150 Years but without Its Historian," andrewfhenderson.com/2020/05/18/pewee-valley-celebrates-150-years-but-without-its-historian.

67. Little Colonel Players, www.littlecolonelnet.

68. The main source for this section is National Register of Historic Places Registration Form (June 23, 1989), "Ashwood Avenue Historic District," available at Pewee Valley Historical Society, "Pewee Valley National Register Properties and Historic Districts," www.peweevalleyhistory.org/national-register.html.

Chapter 7

69. Pewee Valley Historical Society, "William A. Smith House/Olde Pine Tower," www.peweevalleyhistory.org/williamasmith-house.html.

70. "Pewee Valley Store Hit by $6,000 Fire / Telephone Operators Call Anchorage for Aid and Save Building," *Courier-Journal*, November 26, 1928.

71. Pewee Valley Historical Society, "The Sweet Shop at 301 LaGrange Road," www.peweevalleyhistory.org/sweet-shop.html.

72. "3 Hurt in Fight at Pewee Valley," *Courier-Journal*, May 20, 1936.

73. National Register Nomination for St. James Episcopal Church, Pewee Valley Historical Society, www.peweevalleyhistory.org/national-register-st-james.html.

74. Pewee Valley Historical Society, "St. Aloysius Church and Cemetery," www.peweevalleyhistory.org/st-aloysius.html.

75. Ad for the Walker Exchange, *Louisville Courier*, October 18, 1858, 3.

76. "Destructive Fire in Pewee Valley," *Daily Democrat*, December 19, 1863.

77. "Pewee Valley Homes. Ideal Resting Places, Owned by Fortunate Louisville People—Glimpses of Favored Spots," *Courier-Journal*, August 11, 1895.

78. "Egyptian Tomb to Be Built in Louisville," *Middlesboro (Kentucky) Daily News*, March 15, 1923.

79. Pewee Valley Historical Society, "Rosswoods: The Van Horne–Ross House," www.peweevalleyhistory.org/rosswoods.html.

80. "Country Seats. A Pen Picture of Pewee Valley," *Courier-Journal*, December 25, 1871.

81. Pewee Valley Historical Society, "Tanglewood: The Barclay Years and Beyond," www.peweevalleyhistory.org/tanglewood-barclays.html.

82. Pewee Valley Historical Society, "National Register Nomination for the Bondurant-Huston House," www.peweevalleyhistory.org/national-register-bondurant-huston.html.

83. Pewee Valley, "Bondurant-Huston House: Castlewood," www.peweevalleyhistory.org/bondurant-huston-house-castlewood.html.

84. "J.D. Bondurant & Co.," *Courier-Journal*, January 1, 1891, www.peweevalleyhistory.org/bondurant-huston-house-castlewood.html.

85. Pewee Valley Historical Society, "Joseph H. Ellis House," www.peweevalleyhistory.org/joseph-h-ellis-house.html.

86. "The Winter Colony at Pewee Valley," *Courier-Journal*, November 28, 1897.

87. "J.H. Ellis Assumes Duties of New Position," *Courier-Journal*, November 2, 1902.

88. Philemporium Society of the Commercial College of Kentucky University, *Ancestry, Life and Reminiscences of Gen. Wilbur R, Smith* (Lexington, KY: Transylvania Printing Co., 1913).

89. Nomination of the Locust to the National Register of Historic Places, quoted in Pewee Valley Historical Society, "The Locust: In the Beginning and the Rhorer Years," www.peweevalleyhistory.org/the-locust.html.

90. Pewee Valley Historical Society, "The Locust: In the Beginning and the Rhorer Years."

91. Beers & Lanagan Atlas of Pewee Valley (1879), Pewee Valley Historical Society, www.peweevalleyhistory.org/1879-beers--lanagan.html.

92. Katie S. Smith, in her *Pewee Valley: Land of the Little Colonel* (1974), cited in Peewee Valley Historical Society, "African-American Communities: Frazier Town and Stumptown," www.peweevalleyhistory.org/african-american.html.

93. Reproduced in Peewee Valley Historical Society, "African-American Communities: Frazier Town and Stumptown," www.peweevalleyhistory.org/african-american.html.

94. Oldham County Historical Society, *History & Families of Oldham County, Kentucky: The First Century 1824–1924* (Paducah, KY: Turner Publishing, 1996), 260.

95. Peewee Valley Historical Society, "African-American Communities: Frazier Town and Stumptown."

96. "Fire Guts Church Building, History in Pewee Valley," *Courier-Journal*, August 18, 2003, www.peweevalleyhistory.org/pewee-valley-first-baptist-church.html.

Chapter 8

97. "C.C. Page & Company," Wikidata, www.wikidata.org/wiki/Q29015963.

98. Andre Sennwald, "Shirley Temple and Lionel Barrymore in 'The Little Colonel,' the New Film Music Hall," *New York Times*, March 22, 1935.

99. Wikipedia, "List of Countries by Population 1800," www.en.wikipedia.org/wiki/List_of_countries_by_population_in_1800; Wikipedia, "Russian Empire," en.wikipedia.org/wiki/Russian_Empire.

100. Peewee Valley Historical Society, "Books by Annie Fellows Johnston," www.peweevalleyhistory.org/books-by-annie-fellows-johnston.html.

101. Smith, Karl (August 28, 1895–August 7, 1986), Geographicus Rare Antique Maps, www.geographicus.com/P/ctgy&Category_Code=smithkarl.

102. Pewee Valley Historical Society, "Fox Film Scrapbook Prepared for the Production of the 'Little Colonel' Movie Starring Shirley Temple," www.peweevalleyhistory.org/fox-film-scrapbook.html. The scrapbook is preserved in the collections of the Oldham County History Center in LaGrange, Kentucky, oldhamkyhistory.com.

103. Ibid.

104. Pewee Valley Historical Society, "Little Colonel Puzzles & Card Game by the McLoughlin Brothers," www.peweevalleyhistory.org/puzzles.html.

105. Pewee Valley Historical Society, "Little Colonel Dolls," www.peweevalleyhistory.org/dolls.html. Many of the dolls are in the collection of the Pewee Valley Museum, which occupies the former fire station next door to the Pewee Valley Town Hall, www.peweevalleyhistory.org/pewee-valley-museum.html,

106. Sue Lynn McDaniel, "The Little Colonel: A Phenomenon in Popular Literary Culture," April 1, 1991, Western Kentucky University TopSCHOLAR, 3, digitalcommons.wku.edu/cgi/viewcontent.cgi?https redir=1&article=1004&context=dlsc_fac_pub.

107. Ibid., 5.

108. Rice quoted in McDaniel, "Little Colonel," 5.

109. McDaniel, "Little Colonel," 6–7.

110. Ibid., 25.

Epilogue

111. Niche, "Pewee Valley Crime," www.niche.com/places-to-live/pewee-valley-oldham-ky/crime-safety.

112. [Noble Butler,] *Antiquitates Peweeji* (July 4, 1858), www.peweevalleyhistory.org/antiquitates.html.

ABOUT THE AUTHORS

David Russell is a longtime resident of Pewee Valley. A financial advisor, he joined Atlas Brown in 2014 and is executive vice president and head of The Russell Group, a Chartered Retirement Plan Specialist,® and an Accredited Investment Fiduciary.® A 1976 honors graduate of the University of Kentucky's School of Business, he has served on the boards of Family Health Centers, Wellspring, The Louisville Zoo Foundation Bequest Planning Giving Council, and the Alliance of Community Hospices & Palliative Care Services. He still runs Mo Chuisle (Gaelic for "My Pulse"), the Shelby County family farm, which is a working cattle and agricultural operation, as well as a retreat he uses to balance his understanding and appreciation of family assets. He moved, with his wife, Donna, and their two daughters, to Oldham County in 1988 and started their second historic renovation project. Donna, a journalist and marketer by profession, discovered a love of history, became an expert in local history, and dreamed of writing a historical book about Pewee Valley. Her life was cut short in 2019, but she left behind thirty-two gigs of writing and research, which professional writer Alan Axelrod helped David transform into this book.

Alan Axelrod, PhD, is the author of more than 150 books, including *The Gilded Age 1876–1912: Overture to the American Century* (Sterling/Union Square, 2017) and many other works of American history and biography, among them: *In the Time of the Revolution: Living the War of American Independence* (Lyons Press, 2020), *Miracle at Belleau Wood: The Birth of the Modern U.S. Marine Corps* (Revised Edition, 2018), *Lost Destiny: Joe Kennedy Jr. and the Doomed Mission to Save London* (Palgrave Macmillan, 2015), *A Savage Empire: Trappers, Traders, Tribes, and the Wars That Made America* (St. Martin's Press/Thomas Dunne Books, 2011), *The Horrid Pit: The Battle of the Crater, the Civil War's Cruelest Mission* (Carroll & Graf, 2007), and others.

After receiving his PhD in English (specializing in early American literature and culture) from the University of Iowa in 1979, Axelrod taught early American literature and culture at Lake Forest College (Lake Forest, Illinois) and Furman University (Greenville, South Carolina). He then entered scholarly publishing in 1982 as associate editor and scholar with the Henry Francis du Pont Winterthur Museum (Winterthur, Delaware), an institution specializing in the history and material culture of America prior to 1832. Axelrod has been an acquiring editor for several major publishers, and in 1997, he founded The Ian Samuel Group, Inc., a consulting, creative services, editing, and online content provider in Atlanta, where he lives with his wife, the artist Anita Arliss.

Visit us at
www.historypress.com